RECEIVING THE COSMIC CHRIST

The Experience of Global Community

Shahan Jon

KARUNA FOUNDATION

Published by Karuna Foundation, Berkeley, California

Karuna Foundation
P.O. Box 11422
Berkeley, CA 94701-2422
U.S.A.

Library of Congress Catalog Card Number: 89-63583
ISBN 0-9624414-0-6

Printed in the United States of America

THE GREAT EVOCATION

From the point of Light within the Mind of God
Light streams forth into the minds of men.
Light illumines Earth.

From the point of Love within the Heart of God
Love streams forth into the hearts of men.
Christ is now come.
We are One as the Christ.

From the center where the Will of God is known
Purpose guides the little wills of men—
The purpose which the Masters know and serve.

From the center which we call the race of men
The plan of Love and Light works out.

Light and Love and Power now restore the Plan on Earth.

PREFACE

NOW is the moment of the reappearance on Earth of the Christ energy of pure Love. A cycle of time has now begun that holds the opportunity for the Christing of Humanity and Earth.

Humanity has waited thousands of years for this moment. As citizens of Earth, we have the opportunity to here and now consciously unite in love and receive the Cosmic Christ. It is the union into community consciousness which makes the reappearance of the Cosmic Christ possible in our hearts, our societies, and the world community.

The planet has created a time of transformative work for the sake of expressing another level of truth. This is just as in various historic periods when the planet has shifted into a new reality, sometimes through the work of one master teacher, and sometimes through the work done by an entire group mind. In our present cycle, the integration of group minds into community consciousness will create the shift resulting in the expression of another level of truth, a new reality for the planet and all beings that live upon it.

The new reality is already emerging. Within this new reality is the awareness that thoughts may be used as pure energy forms to re-create the experience of consciousness on personal, social, and global levels. Small groups of individuals working in community consciousness may re-create the patterns of identity on all levels to more perfectly express Divinity. Whether this innate spirituality is called the Cosmic Christ, or Buddha-nature, or Great Spirit, or Universal Love, the experience is the same. Humanity now has the opportunity to tap into this new level of awareness and consciously create a global spiritual renaissance.

This book provides guidelines for individuals and groups to experience Christ within, to compassionately unite as One community consciousness, and to re-create patterns of identity on personal, social, and global levels. You may use this book as a manual to consciously link your existing prayer or meditation groups into a global community consciousness of the Christ. Or, you may wish to create a new circle of Light for this purpose. Chapter one will give you the simple guidelines for making full use of *Receiving The Cosmic Christ*.

Thank you for choosing to join with millions of people worldwide as we collectively sound the tone of a new reality and link in love and compassion to receive the Cosmic Christ.

TABLE OF CONTENTS

Receiving the Cosmic Christ

CHAPTER 1

THE EXPERIENCE OF COMMUNITY

YOU'RE invited to share in an adventure that cuts across the boundaries of nationality, culture, race, sex, age, and opinion.

What can be experienced at this time is a force so powerful that it breaks through your presumed limitations and the boundaries of your personal world, a force so profound that it instantly unites everyone and everything. This is the power of the heart, for it is through compassion that we will heal ourselves and our world. In a state of compassion, you can recognize that everyone is a member of one world community.

Compassion is less a change of heart than it is a profound expression of what is already active in you. The collective expression of compassion builds a new world community.

Compassion is a means in your experience for making contact with a new reality. We are moving into a time of a new reality. This new reality is not simply a new age or a change of perspective; it is a birth into a new way of being that will radically transform life on Earth and maintain the experience of community. The collective expression of compassion by Humanity is the reappearance of the Cosmic Christ on Earth.

You may have had at least one experience in your life when, in a group, something remarkable happened; suddenly you felt a profound sense of connection and belonging. All the individuals in the group seemed to join together in such a way that something warm, safe, loving, and very, very special began to be shared. This is the experience of community. In the experience of community, you may begin to experience the Cosmic Christ.

Community can be experienced in a variety of circumstances and settings. Perhaps you have had the experience of community in an organization that is working for a particular cause, or as a member of an athletic team. You may have experienced community through the fellowship of a church. Community might be experienced in a family, a study group, or a weekend workshop of strangers. Sometimes the experience of community is triggered by disaster or war. Perhaps you participated in a war effort and can remember the bond of community you shared with those with whom you lived or by whose side you fought.

*IN THE EXPERIENCE OF COMMUNITY,
YOU MAY KNOW THE COSMIC CHRIST.*

In all the varieties of circumstances and settings in which community may be experienced, the essential experience of community is always the same. Individuals begin to sense and express something that comes from their deepest inner nature. This expression flows from the heart and instantly joins together everyone and everything. The power of the heart is more fundamental and more profound than any distinction, characteristic, belief, or opinion that separates one from another. The power of the heart is the Cosmic Christ.

Take a moment now to remember any experience of community that you have had. Recall how you felt.

Now consider what it would be like to share the experience of community with everyone, all the time, in your life. Consider what it would feel like to live in this world if everyone everywhere shared the experience of community at all times.

We can have this. The experience of community is natural to Humankind. It may not be an ordinary experience in this time of history, but it is a fundamental, natural experience. In fact, the experience of community is natural, and the experience of separation and isolation is unnatural. Community is what you experience when you express and share the deepest part of yourself and appreciate and honor that same essence in everyone else.

Often, when individuals begin to experience community, they attribute it to the context in which it is experienced. They think they are experiencing a certain organization, church, workshop, or a group of special people, for example. They fail to see that the experience of community comes from within themselves. Community can be experienced in any group, in any setting, under any circumstance because community is what results when individuals compassionately share the expression of the deepest human nature.

The first step in creating and sustaining the experience of community is to choose your compassion over your judgment. Compassion is an honest appreciation and respect for whatever is, without the limitation of judgment. When you judge, you separate yourself from what you judge. When you judge yourself, you deny yourself the experience of your own wholeness. When you judge others, you deny yourself the experience of community.

In a state of compassion, you can recognize that what is expressed and shared in community is exactly what is present and active within everyone at all times.

That is why every gathering can be an occasion for the experience of community. Community is not just for the privileged few at select times. Community is sharing the experience of the one inner truth that we all have in common. It is an acknowledgment of what unites us, what has always united everyone. The connection is already present. We need only to express it honestly to share the experience of community.

THE FIRST STEP
IS TO CHOOSE YOUR COMPASSION
OVER YOUR JUDGMENT.

You can start right now to live in the experience of community. You can initiate the experience of community in every gathering and group in which you participate. The experience of community is not something that will come from outside of you. It starts in you. Simply begin to express and share your deepest nature and to honor that in others.

Any group in which you participate may be what I call a core community. Essentially, a core community is a small group of individuals who are aware of their deep spiritual connection with one another and act from the experience of community. This is in distinction to a community where the individuals may or may not be aware of their connection and, consequently, do not act from the experience of community.

You have the opportunity to begin to experience the new reality at this time, if you choose. You may use this book as a tool to assist you in opening into a new experience of yourself. Here we are speaking quite literally of a new experience, not simply a new opinion or idea about yourself. Education in this time of an emerging new reality must be based on experience rather than just idea if it is to be relevant.

YOU HAVE THE OPPORTUNITY TO EXPERIENCE THE NEW REALITY AT THIS TIME.

This book has been prepared as a tool to assist you on a personal level to sense and express your deepest nature, and on a group level, to create the experience of community. The experience of community is a means for Humanity to express the Cosmic Christ. Each chapter has two parts; they are meant to be played with simultaneously. The first part of each chapter is designed for individual use. The second is designed for group experience.

To gain the maximum benefit from this book, read and play with one chapter each week and also meet weekly with a few friends to share an experience of the corresponding group process for that chapter. The second part of this chapter will give you the simple guidelines necessary to take full advantage of this opportunity for group cooperation.

When you truly understand that every gathering of individuals can be an opportunity for experiencing community, you will know that all of Humankind is one community. This is the nature of human consciousness. Consciousness is simply the field of awareness. There is one fundamental consciousness, and it has many aspects. Human consciousness is simply one focus; it is one community in the larger community of consciousness. This is how you may know yourself as individual, and also, as universal.

Within the one consciousness, you are an individual. You are a unique expression of the rich diversity of qualities and characteristics of consciousness. Simultaneously, you are an aspect of human consciousness, and you share a common community awareness with all other human beings. Human consciousness is an aspect of the one consciousness. According to the breadth of your awareness, you may understand yourself to be your personal identity or the All of consciousness. You may understand this as a lake of consciousness; as you stand in the center, you send ripples out in every direction. As your consciousness expands, the ripples of your awareness embrace more of the lake.

Whether or not you are aware of it, you are simultaneously an influence on all levels of consciousness. There is but one consciousness; you are that. There is no separation.

Spirit, the energy that is aware of itself everywhere at all times, joins together everything in the universe. Spirit is consciousness. Consciousness is self-aware energy. Everything that you are and that you perceive in the universe is active, aware energy. Every being, every form, every idea or concept, every event is energy; it is a unique identity that is a pattern of energy.

YOU ARE SPIRIT IN A UNIQUE COMPOSITE OF PATTERNS OF CONSCIOUSNESS.

You yourself are energy. You are one fundamental pattern of energy that is unlimited, eternal, all-wise, ever-vital, as deep self. At the same time, you are many other patterns which represent every belief, every part of your form, every aspect of your identity from a fingernail to your liver, to the patterns of your behavior, to the process of your perception. You are a composite of many energy patterns, and yet, you have one fundamental identity pattern as deep self. Deep self unites and constantly creates, re-creates, and regenerates the various patterns of your experience. Through all of this, the universal pattern of consciousness extends. You are this; you are Spirit in a unique composite of patterns of consciousness.

In community consciousness, as you begin to have the experience of community, something miraculous happens. The identity patterns of all the individuals involved begin to be regenerated. Regeneration is simply the renewal and re-creation of any pattern to more perfectly reflect Divine order. When you begin to sense and express the most fundamental and universal pattern of your identity, other patterns begin to more clearly reflect that basic pattern. For example, what we call healing is simply the regeneration of any, or a number of, personal identity patterns.

The seeds of my own exploration into this area were sown some fifteen years ago. At that time, I had received a grant from the Rockefeller Foundation to create a film about some recent legislation as it concerned the public school system of the United States. I had taken great care to assure that a broad cross-section of cultures, races, and economic groups would be represented; this afforded me the rare opportunity to view the educational system in action in a very broad spectrum. It was a sobering but enlightening experience.

What I realized is that legislation alone cannot create change. I had already discovered through my activities in the peace movement that peace cannot be created while feeling anger. Now it was becoming more and more clear to me that any effective change in society comes about through a profound change of heart, person by person. I realized that the global change I so much desired to see would need to start in me.

This realization launched me into an exploration of myself that unfolded through the human potential movement, meditation, and six years in graduate school studying psychology, Eastern philosophy, and religious traditions. It was during the period as a graduate student that I began to open even more rapidly, often in violent and painful ways. My experiences required me to undertake an in-depth study of the theory and function of energy in both systems of healing and religious experience. My desperate need for guidance was answered when I became a student of Diya, a being identifying itself as an overmind who works for personal and planetary transformation. For two years, I was a student of Diya through the expert intuitive, Richard Ryal.

The materials of this book are to a great extent based on what I learned from Diya and how that learning evolved through a program that I developed called Conscious Linking. In my explorations, I had become increasingly aware that the power of the individual can be focused and amplified through group cooperation. I began to have a vision of a global network of interconnected small groups, which could focus the power of all the individuals involved for maximum personal, social, and planetary transformation. In my work as a human development consultant, I began to create such groups and to further develop the techniques of consciously linking these groups into a global network of consciousness.

Since that time, my vision has become more expanded and clarified. I now realize the nature and the potential of the experience of community. I have come to realize that small groups of individuals—as core communities united into a global network of core communities—can quite literally focus the power of everyone involved to regenerate the energy patterns of consciousness on a personal level, on a social level, and on a planetary level. I have come to understand that by regenerating the energy patterns of consciousness on every level—re-creating all patterns to more perfectly reflect their innate spirituality—Humanity can be the vehicle for a total manifestation of the Cosmic Christ on Earth.

WE MAY RE-CREATE
THE ENERGY PATTERNS OF CONSCIOUSNESS
TO EXPRESS THE COSMIC CHRIST
ON EARTH.

The processes and techniques in this book were developed and tested in small groups over a period of eight years. They are tools with which you may regenerate the patterns of your own life, and through group cooperation and the experience of community, global patterns of experience. They are tools with which we may all compassionately unite to express the Cosmic Christ.

This regeneration is possible because all patterns are aware energy, and they all interact. They are aspects of the one consciousness. As any pattern on any level or of any magnitude is regenerated, the entire field of consciousness is realigned and transformed. When you heal a small cut on your finger, you contribute to the regeneration of universal consciousness. Nothing acts outside the whole. Nothing is separate. Everything is an aspect of the one self-aware energy.

Everything is in relationship. Everything is in community. You may understand these patterns of self-aware energy to be grouped as communities of consciousness. An organ in your body may be understood as a community of cells. Your body may be understood as a community of consciousness that includes all the organs and systems of the body. There are communities within communities within communities. There are communities of atoms and cells and organs within any individual identity. There is a community of individuals within any species. There are communities of species that compose the greater plant and animal communities. The communities of minerals, plants, animals, and Humankind together form the world community.

Planetary consciousness is simply the community of all the various identities of our world. This world community is constantly being created and re-created through the regeneration of every pattern of consciousness within it.

We are moving into a time of a new reality for Earth.

As we begin to awaken to the fact that we are not separate, we begin to live in the experience of community. We begin to express more clearly the most basic identity pattern of spirit that flows through each of us and everything. This regenerates the identity patterns in your personal life, and through group cooperation, it regenerates on the social and planetary levels.

This is why the effect is so profound as we act from the experience of community. You may choose to work and meditate individually, and you can create the experience of regeneration in your own life; this will have an effect on the whole. But in community, the field of consciousness in which you have active awareness is greatly expanded. That is why group cooperation amplifies the power of regeneration and very profoundly affects consciousness on the social and planetary levels, as well as the personal. We have the opportunity for group cooperation that will transform the planetary consciousness and build a new world community, one that expresses the Cosmic Christ.

This is a time of great opportunity for you. You are not simply witnessing the changes in the world in this time of planetary transformation; you are taking part in this transformation because you are a member of the world community.

Transformation is simply a rearrangement of the patterns through which consciousness identifies itself. At this time, the identity patterns of everything and everyone in the world community are being re-created, and this is planetary transformation. All of the patterns of consciousness that compose your identity are also being re-created, and this is personal transformation. Personal transformation is one part of planetary transformation.

TRANSFORMATION IS
A REARRANGEMENT OF THE PATTERNS
THROUGH WHICH CONSCIOUSNESS IDENTIFIES ITSELF.

As you understand what transformation is, you will realize that the problems we face are not our primary challenge. This time of transformation is not intended ultimately to solve the problems of society, which are inherent in our current state of consciousness. The primary challenge in planetary consciousness is to move to a new state by regenerating all the patterns of consciousness in the world community. This rearrangement of the patterns of consciousness on every level of the world community will accelerate over the end of this century and culminate in a new reality for the planet and all the creatures that live upon it. The new reality holds the possibility of a full Christing of Humanity and Earth.

A network of core communities is being created to assist this process of regeneration as we collectively move into the experience of a new reality. The core community network is not an organization to join. It is a network of communities that are choosing to work and play in consciousness with each other to focus and amplify the effectiveness of everyone and every community involved and create maximum transformation on every level of the world community. You are invited to share in the wonder and the adventure of group cooperation as we move together into a new reality. By creating a core community and practicing the processes and principles of regeneration which are shared in this book, you will have the tools with which you can repattern consciousness on a personal level, on a social level, and on a planetary level. The second part of this chapter will give you the simple guidelines to begin your group work and play.

This is a time to celebrate our union as one world community. We have the opportunity to begin to have the experience of community that cuts across the boundaries of nationality, race, culture, sex, age, opinion, and even species. I invite you to begin to live the vision of a global community of individuals who are united through the power of the heart. Through compassion, we will all be uplifted and healed. Through compassion, we will regenerate the world community. Through compassion, the powerful expression of what is true in the very depths of yourself, we will begin to step into the next levels of awareness for Humankind and express the Cosmic Christ. We will share what is truly a new reality of fulfillment and joy. Let yourself open to a new experience of yourself, of ourself, in community through the power of your own heart, compassion.

*LET YOURSELF OPEN TO THE COSMIC CHRIST
THROUGH THE EXPERIENCE OF COMMUNITY.*

Group Process 1: The Core Community

Your core community may be any existing small group, or you may wish to create a new group. To begin, gather about eight people who wish to share the experience of community. These people may be neighbors, friends, co-workers, members of organizations or a church to which you belong, or strangers. The only bonding factor necessary is that you each wish to share this experience. This is your core community.

Your core community will meet weekly for best results. Most likely, you will need to select one evening at a time when all your core community members can always gather for a period of a least two hours.

You will want to meet in a comfortable environment in which you will not be disturbed or interrupted. Frequently, core communities meet in a member's home, and this can be alternated.

As you first begin your core community, there will be a number of details to be decided. Keep in mind that your purpose is to create through a core community. Your goal is not to create a group. Keep it simple so that you are not distracted from your real purpose.

Each week you will have an opportunity to generate group experiences. The guidelines and processes for your weekly gatherings are meant to complement the text. It is important that each person read the desig-

nated chapter for the week and play with those processes in preparation for the weekly gathering.

At your weekly core community gathering, one person will be the facilitator. Your community will need to select a person to act as facilitator in advance of the gathering. This is a role that all members may wish to share on a rotating basis. Prior to the community gathering, the weekly facilitator will read and play with the materials designed for groups, which appear at the end of each chapter, to be prepared to guide the group session.

Each weekly gathering has a simple format. In the first several gatherings while the community is just forming, you will want to simply introduce yourselves, make some organizational decisions, and experience the group process that is provided for that particular gathering. By chapter four, "Integrating as Community," your core community should have resolved the logistical details including who will be the continuing members of the community.

The basic format of each weekly gathering beginning in chapter four has four main parts:

First, your core members integrate as a community. This process is taught in chapter four, and you will need to always begin each group session with an alignment. Once you have experienced this a number of times, it may not be necessary to guide the group through the process as it is written in chapter four. Every core community will find its own style and preferences. Some may prefer a period of silence during which time community members may consciously integrate as community; other communities may want to continue a verbal guided process and even add music. The length of time devoted to this initial process of integration will depend entirely upon the individuals in the community. There is no one ideal format; each community will use what works for it at the time, and this is likely to develop and change as the community becomes more adept at this work. The important point is that the integration as community must be accomplished, by whatever procedure, at the beginning of each community gathering.

Second, take some time for sharing and reporting experiences that community members have had throughout the week working and playing with the weekly chapter and materials.

Third, the weekly facilitator guides the community through the group process, which is provided at the end of each chapter. The processes are written so that they may guide the community through experiences.

The processes should be read very slowly, with many pauses. They are written so that a long pause or an extended few minutes of silence comes at the end of every paragraph. Each process should take twenty to thirty minutes, or considerably longer. If the facilitator is also fully participating in the process with the group, rather than simply reading or trying to guide, the timing of the process will seem natural and be effective. If you wish, you may use these techniques with music. The facilitator should be well-prepared with the materials in advance of the gathering. It is generally not a good idea to discuss the experience of the process immediately after its completion; this limits and stops the experience.

Fourth is a period of celebration. Frequently, an environment of great healing and power is created through this work and play, and it can be very beneficial for community members to just be in the environment in light social contact for a period after the group session. This time is an opportunity to compassionately experience the rich diversity and uniqueness of all the individual personalities in your community. Wonderful community experiences happen sitting in a circle and sharing tea and cookies after a session. Of course, birthdays and holidays are cause for more shared celebration. Each community will need to decide what is appropriate to it and what it wants to create. A word of warning to the host or hostess: no one ever wants to go home! So make sure that some time considerations are discussed. Also, keep it simple and share the responsibilities. The purpose is to extend the experience of healing and celebration with ease and joy. This can be an important part of your core community experience.

Your weekly core community gathering will probably last about two-and-a-half hours, perhaps from 7-9:30 or 7:30-10 in the evening. It is essential that all members be committed to the community and be prompt because the community cannot properly generate a group consciousness without all the members present at the beginning of the session, and this defeats and limits the purpose of your core community.

Through your core community, you have the opportunity to create and share something wondrous. It is your attitude of wonder and adventure that will begin to fill your life with miracles.

CHAPTER 2

BUILDING A NEW WORLD COMMUNITY

THE new world community is the result that comes from transforming your own life. As you and other individuals repattern your individual consciousness, the world community is transformed. You and your communities build a new world community as you begin to express compassion and share the experience of community.

This is a time to be in a new way. The new reality is not about a change of opinion or perspective. It is a regeneration of your current life as a new state and a new experience of yourself. This can most easily be accomplished in groups. When groups have community consciousness, it is possible to move beyond the belief systems and presumed limitations of any one individual.

By joining together through the experience of community consciousness, those who are willing to step into the next levels of human awareness are able to access the greater planetary patterns of consciousness in the world community. This is important because all regeneration is created off existing energy patterns.

Regeneration is something that will be explained in depth only after you have been guided through the experience so that you may fully comprehend. For now, simply understand that through community, you are able to access greater planetary energy patterns, which may be re-created.

Much of the change of consciousness for Humankind will occur through the physical sensation of awareness rather than logical thought or idea. The next level of human awareness will first be experienced largely as sensation. Once you have integrated these awarenesses at a cellular level within your body, you will be able to experience them as ideas. This is why the work of the core community network must be based, at this time, on the generation of the sensation—the direct physical experience of energy as a new level of consciousness—rather than analysis and ideas. This is also why many of the discussions of regeneration may seem abstract and elusive to you. Only after you have begun to experience new states of awareness as sensation can you move into the realm of idea.

THE NEXT LEVEL OF HUMAN AWARENESS WILL BE EXPERIENCED FIRST AS SENSATION.

Most of the chapters of this book are designed to guide you into the maximum experience with a minimum of discussion. Only in the later chapters, after you have had a certain level of experience, is explanation offered that can be grasped and that will enhance your awareness rather than serve as a distraction.

Focus your attention in upon yourself now, and give yourself permission to experience a brief and simple exploration of that consciousness at this time.

Allow yourself to be receptive to whatever is appropriate for you. Relax, and understand that it is easier to experience new levels of consciousness when you are strong and accepting.

Look within yourself, and begin to follow the pattern of your breathing as you relax.

The process of breathing is a process of direct access to the power of Spirit, energy that is aware of itself, everywhere at all times. The atmosphere is charged with the presence of Spirit. Each time you inhale, you are drawing Spirit into the body. Each time you exhale, you are sending Spirit back out into the universe. As you breathe, you enliven the Spirit that is within you, that always fills you. You can make the Spirit strong within you by remaining aware of this as you breathe.

Experiencing Spirit, the energy that joins together everything and everyone in the universe, is as simple as experiencing the process of breathing.

Become aware now of the vibration of energy as you inhale.

As you draw air into your lungs, feel the rush of air, and feel the change of vibration in your lungs.

As you exhale, feel the difference in the area of your lungs. Become more sensitive to the energy level as it shifts.

As you inhale again, feel the change of intensity. As you exhale, notice what you feel.

Take a moment to find a pattern of deep, rhythmic breathing. Simply notice your experience.

Paying attention to your breath will be useful to you for adjusting the state of consciousness in which you operate. As you begin to have experiences of more intensified awareness through work and play in your core community, your simple deep, rhythmic breathing will help you to stabilize new levels of consciousness and integrate them on a cellular level within your body.

As you accept what is truly a change in consciousness rather than a change in opinion, your physical body will go through changes. Consciousness is only effective when it is integrated into the cellular structure, not simply of the brain, but of your entire body. The most effective levels of consciousness are those that vibrate throughout the entire cellular structure.

The process of regenerating energy patterns, which you will learn in this book and experience through your participation in a core community, is such that you will be able to integrate new levels of consciousness on a cellular level within yourself and refocus your identity patterns to create any healing that is appropriate to you in an easy and pleasurable way. It is not necessary to go through experiences of violent release and painful openings as you experience and integrate new levels of awareness.

AS YOU ACCEPT A CHANGE IN YOUR CONSCIOUSNESS, YOUR PHYSICAL BODY WILL CHANGE.

As you bring about shifts in consciousness, be alert to your body's needs. Eat what your body desires and finds pleasurable, not what seems distasteful but the mind considers to be helpful. Sometimes the body needs to sleep a great deal, sometimes it will resist all efforts to sleep. Do not blame your body or new states of awareness. Simply witness and accept as you transform.

One of the most powerful ways of anchoring new levels of consciousness, especially if you are having difficulty, is to go into nature. Find a place in nature where you like to be in which you can directly touch the dirt, the rocks, and the plants. Or simply stand in the elements; feel the wind, the rain, or sunshine on your body. If you cannot go to places in nature, you may carry parts of the planet with you. Carry a stone, a leaf, or a flower to touch.

Turn your attention inward once again now, and establish a pattern of deep, rhythmic breathing.

Focus your attention at a point in the back of your skull, where the brain and the spinal column meet. Notice what you feel.

Notice that with your attention, this area becomes active.

Become aware of the vibration, the sensation, that you are experiencing here, at a point where your brain and your spine meet.

Simply feel the vibration at this point, like a ball of energy.

This is a point of emerging group consciousness and community awareness. There is much that will be said and experienced in later chapters about the new awareness that is coming in at this point. But for now, it is most important to simply be aware of the sensation and the vibration here, where your spine and the back of your brain meet.

THE POINT
WHERE YOUR BRAIN AND SPINAL COLUMN MEET IS A FOCUS OF EMERGING COMMUNITY CONSCIOUSNESS.

Focus now upon a point in the front half of your brain, right behind the center of your forehead. Notice that you can begin to breathe through this point. As you do, become aware of the vibration, the sensation, that begins to grow.

Breathe deeply. Notice that you can stimulate and amplify the vibration here as though you were turning up its volume.

Begin to inhale now, as though you were inhaling from the back base of your skull.

As you inhale from the back of your skull, feel the vibration, the active energy, in the front of the brain being pulled further and further back through the brain.

As you feel it begin to cross the midsection of your brain, notice the way the energy vibration changes. Feel the shift in your consciousness. Feel the sensation.

Continuing to breathe deeply and rhythmically, inhaling from the point at the back of your skull, feel the sensation of awareness where your brain and your spinal column meet. Stay with this a few moments.

Now become aware of the sensation in your hands, in the palms of your hands, and in your fingers.

Notice how the vibration here in your hands is being tuned to the vibration at the top of your spine. Notice that you can simply allow this; you do not need to try to do anything. Stay with this as long as you like.

This is more than a preparation for the new level of consciousness you seek. This is actually a first step. We will work more with this in other chapters and offer explanations after you have had a certain level of experience.

By working with this point at the back of your skull, you will be able to open to community consciousness. In turn, your experience of community consciousness develops continuous awareness.

Maintaining continuous awareness rather than periodic awareness is a great challenge in the development of human consciousness at this time. Periodic thinking is the tendency to go from one thought to another. In periodic thinking, you see your own purpose as beginning at one definite point and ending at another. In periodic awareness, you perceive your awareness as something that fills various forms in your life. But in continuous awareness, you understand your awareness to be a force that flows through all the forms of your life.

Through periodic awareness, patterns of thinking become disruptive to forms. On an engineering level, you know that various sound waves go through structures at different frequencies and rhythms and so can be debilitating to a structure. Your mind, because it generates thought which is fundamentally active energy, is capable of being debilitating to your body and the patterns of your life.

Humankind has been cultivating periodic awareness. This has been appropriate. But we are seeing in our world what can happen when the other, continuous, aspect of consciousness is neglected. You will tend to see the disruption of structures and systems when you witness the events of total periodic mind activity on large social scales.

In community consciousness, the various periodic patterns of thinking of all the individuals become attuned. The result is that more sustained thought patterns are generated within the community, and continuous awareness begins to be developed. The community consciousness gathers together what is common in all the various minds in the community and creates a broader awareness.

Even if your core community can generate continuous, uninterrupted community consciousness for a period of only five minutes in these early phases of your core community, the members of your community will become aware of what seems to be innovative, and yet, is the next reasonable step of action for individual members, for your community, and for Humankind. The next level of human creativity will evolve through continuous awareness. In community consciousness, you are able to most easily develop continuous awareness.

Continuous consciousness was once active in Humankind. Now it is an awareness that Humankind is beginning to retrieve as a community. Through this cycle of planetary transformation, some old levels of awareness that have not been currently active will be awakened and aligned with new levels of awareness that have not yet been expressed by the human community on Earth.

You may think of some of these levels of consciousness as hibernating within you. Now it is time to awaken and express the consciousness of a new reality as it emerges through you and the entire planetary consciousness. You have the opportunity to begin to express this new awareness now. The choice is yours. The changes of this time of transformation have already begun.

YOU HAVE THE OPPORTUNITY
TO EXPRESS NEW AWARENESS NOW.

A single core community eventually creates ripples of awareness throughout human consciousness. This makes it possible in the field of human consciousness to create resonance with others who may also benefit. This principle has been beautifully demonstrated by the Transcendental Meditation Sidhis Program; in that program, teams of meditators have been sent to trouble spots in the world and have simply practiced their meditation programs in hotels and the violence in that area has diminished.

At this time, we are building an extended community of transformation. This extended community is simply a field of consciousness in which all involved are actively aware of their deep spiritual connection with one another. The extended community is the community consciousness of all the many small groups who are compassionately creating the experience of community. The extended community is a vehicle for the manifestation of universal love, the Cosmic Christ. The purpose of this community is the transformation of consciousness, the generation of a new experience of identity for the entire world community.

YOU ARE A MEMBER OF A COMMUNITY
THAT INCLUDES ALL LIFE ON EARTH
AND THROUGHOUT THE UNIVERSE.

In doing this work, you are connected with other communities on Earth and on other levels of reality. Do not see yourself simply as a link in a horizontal family that extends across the surface of Earth throughout human society. You are also part of a vertical community. Vertical communities unite species and levels of reality. You are a member of a vertical community that includes all life on Earth and throughout our universe. Vertical communities generate the greater awareness of transformation. They are the stabilizing forces of universal transformation.

Our planet is not the only focus of transformation in the universe at this time by any means. Its process runs parallel and sometimes intertwines directly with other focuses within our universe. We affect them just as they affect us. The entire universe is in a state of transformation, and we are creating all of this together.

There is a specific opportunity for group cooperation at this time. Your participation in a core community provides you the opportunity to draw upon the power of your community for personal healing and development, and to be an active agent of planetary transformation. In active community consciousness, it is possible for the community as a whole to grasp a great deal more awareness than most of the individuals involved would be able to generate alone and sustain on their own.

All of this is possible because there is one fundamental pattern of consciousness extending throughout everything at all times. This is Source. Source is the awareness and power that motivates any individual, any lifetime, any form, anything that can be perceived or conceived of in experience. Source is what is essential, what is essence in yourself and anyone else. Source is the one pattern that is continuous and constant. Source is the identity pattern that you share with all others; it is what makes regeneration possible on a personal level, on a social level, on a planetary level, and throughout the entire universe.

Consider who you are to have Source within you. Consider what you can express that is far more than you believe yourself to be or believe you can be. The source of the new world community is within us.

THE SOURCE OF THE NEW WORLD COMMUNITY IS WITHIN US.

Group Process 2: Getting Started

As your core community is just forming, you will need to devote yourselves to resolving some of the initial details of organization and becoming acquainted.

Use this session as an opportunity to introduce yourselves, to become acquainted, and to answer some of the practical questions involved such as where you will be meeting and how you will handle facilitation.

Then take a period of about twenty minutes to meditate, either in silence or with music, focusing on the point at the back of the skull, where the brain and the spinal column meet.

CHAPTER 3

STARTING WITH THE SELF

COMPASSION for yourself is the starting point of your transformation. Being who you are is a great advantage to you. Whatever you may gain from doing what improves your life or expands your awareness always comes from exactly who you are now. That is why it is crucial for you to appreciate who you are, rather than trying in any transformative work to be something or someone that you wish you would become someday.

Aspirations are powerful motivators for learning and creating, but images that are in any way based on a lack of faith in who you are now will not serve you. Such images imply a lack of belief in your own greatness. Greatness is not something that you build over time. You may build awareness of your greatness, but greatness is an inherent quality. It is a quality of your essence. You cannot truly become great; you can only finally become aware of your own greatness, your own Christ consciousness, and express it honestly.

All of your true aspirations are firmly rooted in who you already are. Images of who you want to be that are based on a presumption that you are not yet this person come from the desire to measure yourself according to what and who you think others are.

All that the new reality can be on the planet is already present in you. All that will be effective at this time for you is simply what can clear away any dedication you have to who you think you ought to be. It is when you clear away all you ought to be that you can finally see who you are.

It is through what you consider to be your successes and your failures that you have created much of the form of your identity. But you did not create the content of your identity from either success or failure. It cannot be done. The form of your identity is your personality and all the aspects of your life that are continually changing, but the content of your identity is constant. The content of your identity is your essence. You cannot create content in identity. You can enhance your awareness of content in your identity, but the content is already present. All you can do with the greatest of your hopes and the greatest of your doubts is to change the form of your identity. Who you are inherently will never be shifted through success or failure.

As you realize that you cannot change the content of your identity but can only enhance, expand, diminish, or limit your experience of this content, you will understand why it is important in any transformative work to be fully dedicated to, and appreciative of, who you already are. All of your learning and growth comes from recognizing more clearly what is already within you.

ACCEPT YOURSELF WITH COMPASSION AND YOU WILL REALIZE WHO YOU ALREADY ARE.

Accept yourself as appropriate at this time, and you will begin to notice your own essence. You can simply be at your best. You will never need to be what you call "perfect" to be at your best. You are already perfect, even if you cannot perceive it. Your life is a continual refinement and unfolding expression of what is already perfect. Your personality and the challenges that are unique to your life are simply the ever-changing tools through which you learn and express yourself.

Being at your best will be your experience only if you can accept yourself for who you are in the present. It does not matter what your strengths and weaknesses are. The more you are willing to appreciate yourself with compassion rather than judgment, the more you will be able to assess what is happening in your life.

Transformation taps what is universal. We will be speaking more of these universal energies and how to use them in later chapters. At this point, it is important for you to realize that the universal energies that can be tapped for generating powerful healing and transformation are uplifting to those who have compassion for themselves and others, and eventually are debilitating to those whose priority is judgment over compassion.

THE POSSIBILITIES FOR THE MOST PROFOUND TRANSFORMATION COME FROM COMPASSION.

Who you are at this time, the whole of yourself—form and content—is what makes it possible for you to realize that healing is possible, and that you have a role in planetary transformation.

In the world community, a great deal of individual healing needs to be done, as well as a great deal of group healing. The small core groups—as communities empowered by their union into one global vehicle for the Cosmic Christ—are likely to have a very significant impact. But we cannot have strong core communities without strong individuals in the community.

Individuals who believe that being strong comes from being right or being more skilled can be a weakness in the community. There is far more strength in compassion than in judgment. This is what brings a core community of strong individuals together. In the state of compassion, you are able to recognize that others can be loved no matter what their faults, and also that others can be loved and not envied no matter what their strengths.

COMPASSION IS WITHOUT JUDGMENT.

Compassion is a state by which two masters appreciate each other. Compassion is without judgment. In compassion, you do not demand of yourself that everyone and everything be loved by you. Compassion is an honest appreciation and respect for yourself and all others without judgment.

Imagine, if you will, a core community in which everyone actively involved has achieved some level of broad personal compassion. Imagine what such a core community can experience when those involved love each other, not despite themselves and despite each other, but exactly because of each other. In such a core community, people's personal problems and limitations are neither indulged in nor treated as weakness, but seen as the opportunity for more healing and transformation, and further occasion for fulfillment and celebration.

The possibilities for the most profound healing and transformation come from compassion. The very essence of the Cosmic Christ is compassion. In a core community, it is crucial that compassion be understood and appreciated as an act of power. Compassion is not a cure for insecurities, judgments, or weakness. Compassion is a willingness to believe that you have a place in the universe because of who you already are. If this is true of you, it must also be true of all others. True compassion is a state of great personal power.

COMPASSION IS AN ACT OF POWER.

When you deal with others compassionately, you deal with them in total respect from a state of total self-respect. It is healing simply to be in the presence of those who are truly compassionate. Such people will serve a great creative purpose in this time of transformation. We will be working directly with developing presence in later chapters.

In a state of compassion, you realize that nothing specific is necessary for you to do or be. Rather, it is important simply to delight in the possibilities of healing and transformation, to delight in the process, and to be uplifted by what you do.

What is true of the individual is also true of the core community if it is to be a strong one. A community of such people is a ring of light, a ring of power. Such a core community can correct the apparent problems of the world in which this group lives and works. Core communities united on such a level of consciousness are able to generate a specific, powerful thoughtform in the world community. For any core community and the global core community network to create results that will be an inspiration, they must contribute not only to what seem to be the solutions to world problems, but must contribute powerfully to the planetary consciousness. By acting from the state of compassion, the core community network contributes the thoughtforms of love, acceptance, and compassion. By acting from the state of compassion, the core community network is a pure expression of the Cosmic Christ.

The great healing that is being generated in our world is not for fixing what is wrong; it is for enhancing the awareness of what is true. What is right and what is wrong is not the same as what is true. What is true is what is constant. It is the constant spiritual ground of the entire universe. In a state of compassion, you can recognize the one constant, fundamental pattern of consciousness that is at the heart of everything in the universe, Spirit.

COMPASSION EXPRESSES THE COSMIC CHRIST.

You have an opportunity to participate in the creation of a core community that is an integral part of a global community of transformation that synthesizes the consciousness of individuals without limiting individuality. In a core community, you know the unity of Humankind through the experience of community, and you simultaneously celebrate and compassionately honor the rich diversity of individuality which is human.

You can create a core community that will have a great deal of impact upon the planet. But do not try simply to create a community; rather, create through a core community. The core community must not be the result of your efforts. Let your community be the means by which your effort can be rewarded for the delight and satisfaction of all those involved. If you will do this, you must do this as strong individuals, not necessarily as individuals who are the best trained, nor able to create the best results, but rather as people who are strong enough to be true to themselves.

Perhaps now you are having some doubts about your capabilities and your worthiness. Perhaps you doubt that you can create a core community or act from compassion. You can use your doubt. It is responsible of you to question your abilities and then to find out whether you have the capabilities within yourself. But to continually dwell in doubt is to deny your own resources. It is being like one who is in the wilderness and thirsty and hears the sound of a stream nearby, but sits down and considers, "Am I really hearing a stream?", rather than going to the stream! Doubt and questioning are only appropriate and responsible to the degree that you are willing to follow them and find out whether they are true. If you use your doubt to limit your experience, how will you ever know if your doubt was justified?

It is not productive to question your abilities to the degree that you are not growing, or that you become discouraged. Consider the concept of being dis-couraged. Consider that courage cannot be taken away from you. It can only be diminished by surrendering it. To be courageous, even to be willing to prove that you are unworthy, is a far more creative state than to believe that perhaps you are capable, but you will not see that capability in action.

The core community is a context in which you can share personal and planetary transformation. Through the core community, you have an opportunity to heal by transforming afflicted energy—that which is not appropriate to its context—into creative and generative energy. Such healing is helping to anchor the new reality as it is generated.

It is the integration of the various identities, the unique inclinations, and the diverse skills that is most compelling in these communities. The primary challenge is to sustain compassion through the interaction of all these unique individuals. With compassion, community members are served, and there is an outer expression of the community, the expression of the Cosmic Christ to the entire world community.

THE WORLD COMMUNITY
IS SUSTAINED BY DIVERSITY.

Here will be the point of weakness of the current healing and New Age communities that will fall by the wayside in this time of planetary transformation. The communities that will not endure through the cycle of transformation will be those that are dedicated more to the perpetuation of their own identity than to coordination of global community-consciousness.

The world community is sustained by the varieties of personalities, the varieties of disposition, the varieties of aesthetic orientations within it. The groups that will best survive an era of transition and help to found an identity of a new reality will be those, always, of strong individuals who are brought together by mutual dedication rather than by an agreement or dogma. Dogma is not effective for serving the greater well-being of all consciousness. We have already found in our history that no one dogma has been created that has served the entire world community. There have been spiritual teachers and leaders, sources of great inspiration and creativity, who have touched upon applications of universal truths. But a dogma in itself does not tend to be oriented toward the entire planetary consciousness.

A spiritual awareness within the global community must be an awareness that applies to all those involved: the humans, the animals, the plants, and the minerals. Those who are especially conscious of these roles are essential for a global community that can help introduce the knowledge and creativity for the new reality. This is why the diversity of those involved must be emphasized, and why it is necessary for you to have compassion for those who have different beliefs from you, but nevertheless, have a great deal to contribute to such a community.

You may be strongly challenged by working with a diversity of people, but you may use this as a challenge to be committed to your own truth. If you are willing to believe in your truth, your beauty, your strength and power, you will not expend all of your energy trying to improve what is already appropriate. You will have more attention to dedicate to the transformation for which the community has been founded. You can continue to refine those aspects of yourself that are not desirable to you, but develop to express more fully and clearly who you are.

It is crucial for you to understand this in preparation of work that we will be capable of doing together using profound universal energies. This level of awareness is important in personal development before you work deeply with these universal energies. If you create areas in your identity that you do not believe in, or cannot love, you will not receive the full satisfaction of which you are capable in using these profound energies.

The most crucial step toward developing a true self-love is a relentless dedication to your own truth. When you are willing to see what you consider the worst and the best in you with exactly the same spirit, you will know that you are experiencing self-love. It is a dedication to truth. You must be willing to see all aspects of who you are and accept them all equally.

Your life is a masterpiece in progress, no matter how reluctantly you sustain your identity of mastery. You do not need to wait until you have mastered everything before you express your mastery. This is a profound healing awareness to bring to your core community.

YOU ARE HERE AT THIS TIME OF PLANETARY TRANSFORMATION BECAUSE OF WHO YOU ALREADY ARE.

Behind all of what we do at this time, there is a sense of great purpose. This purpose is within you. You are not here because of what you lack or what you seek. You are here at this time of planetary transformation because of what you have. You are here to do transformative work because of your attributes, your talents, and because of challenges that you will find fulfilling. You need to be reminded occasionally that Spirit is already within you. The opportunity, the new world, the new reality, whatever it is you feel you are seeking, is already within you. That is why you are here.

You must understand that you as an individual have a powerful impact in the world, and through the core community this impact is amplified throughout the planetary consciousness. At this time, the energy field of the planet is being amplified. The vibration of the planet is being increased to meet that of the new reality which is beginning to manifest. The vibration will have a dramatic build-up throughout the end of this century. Our technology, especially the current communication technologies and energy reactors of any kind are building up consciousness of a higher vibration that contributes to the shifting planetary field.

You may begin to understand now a purpose that is served by some aspects of our technology that may be considered dangerous, and how this purpose may be served by other means that may more fully integrate with the planet.

For example, consider the existence of nuclear arms as a presence of powerful energy on the planet. Nuclear weapons are by nature focal points of concentrated high-intensity energy. They concentrate a great deal of energy that, had it been aimed directly into society rather than into machines that are set apart, could have already caused all the devastation for which these weapons are feared. Nuclear weapons are contributing to the build-up of the vibration of the planet. Yet, they are a low-efficiency means for this because they do not integrate with the planet when used. But you, and anyone else, may create energy states in the planet which also increase the vibration.

Through your core community and the amplified power of the network of core communities, you may create energy states in the planetary consciousness that can replace and eliminate the presence of nuclear weapons. You may satisfy the planet's need for higher vibration through your own life and the transformative work of your community. A core community of about eight people can generate enough energy to neutralize a powerful weapon, but this energy must not simply be generated; it must be sustained. The sustenance is crucial, and this is why the development of continuous consciousness in Humankind is so important at this time.

YOU MAY CREATE
ENERGY STATES IN THE PLANETARY CONSCIOUSNESS
THAT REPLACE NUCLEAR WEAPONS.

So that you may begin to understand your power as a consciousness generator more fully, turn your attention inward upon yourself now. Begin to relax, and to establish a pattern of deep, steady breathing.

Allow your awareness now to focus at the top of the head. Feel your consciousness like a ball of light here at the top of your head.

As you continue to breathe deeply and rhythmically, begin to breathe through this ball of light at the top of your head. Feel the sensation. Notice how it increases as you breathe through this point.

Now see this light as being very much like the Earth itself contained in the top of your head.

Allow it to drift with its weight, down from the top of your head, slowly in a line through your body towards the base of your spine until it seems to come to rest along this route. Simply allow this ball of light to come to rest somewhere between the top of your head and the base of your spine.

Notice that you can feel it fitting in this place much like an egg fits a nest.

As you feel this ball of light resting within you, begin to breathe through this point. Notice how the vibration becomes active and lively. Stay with this awhile and allow the power of your breath and your attention to activate this point.

Notice that you can allow the vibration from this point to continue to grow, expand, and begin to fill your entire body. Feel this vibration as sensation beginning to radiate outward and to inhabit your entire body now.

Continuing to breathe deeply and steadily through the ball of radiant energy resting somewhere along the path between the top of your head and the base of your spine, allow it now to flow smoothly and equally throughout your entire body.

Feel the vibration as active power at the top of your head, the tips of your fingers, the tips of your toes, the base of your spine, and all places in between. Stay with this awhile.

If you find it difficult to maintain this intensified vibration, or if you find your body becoming restless when it is filled with this vibration, it is simply a sign that Spirit is beginning to flow and be received in new ways. Allow yourself to deeply and fully experience your activated consciousness throughout your entire body. Stay with this experience as long as you like.

UNIVERSAL TRANSFORMATION STARTS WITH THE SELF.

You are a powerful resource to the world community exactly as you are. If you wish to create a powerful focus of consciousness in the planetary awareness so that nuclear weapons, or weapons of any kind, or institutions of any kind may be replaced, you may do so as you act from the power of who you already are. You are worthy, and you have the opportunity to share yourself deeply with a core community, with a global community of transformation, and with the entire world community. The universal transformation of our time all starts with the self.

Group Process 3: Opening the Heart

As your community is still in its formative stages, continue the process of getting acquainted and answering organizational questions. By the end of this session, and before next week when you will learn to integrate as a community, it should be clear who is committed to participating in your core community.

One group process is provided here. Starting next week, you will begin the regular session format of (1) community alignment, (2) sharing, (3) process, and (4) celebration. This week according to your preference, you may begin or end with the following process:

Take a few deep breaths, and begin to feel the stress and the tension of the day fade away.

Simply allow any thoughts to fade and pass as you begin to experience a sense of relaxation and renewal.

Begin now to breathe very deeply and rhythmically and establish a pattern of easy, deep, steady breathing. Stay with this a few moments.

Notice the sense of relaxation that you are beginning to experience now across your chest and shoulders, down your arms and in your neck, face, abdomen, lower back and legs.

Feel the pleasure of relaxation throughout your entire body as you bring your full attention to present time and present place.

Now bring your attention to your heart center. Notice that you can begin to very gently and easily breathe through your heart.

As you continue to breathe deeply and rhythmically through the center of your heart, notice how the sensation begins to grow, and intensify. Allow yourself to feel your own heart energy as it becomes active.

Feel the sensation as it continues to grow, and notice that you can experience this much like a sphere of radiance, a sphere of warmth, that continually expands from the center of your heart.

Give yourself permission to fully experience the sensation of your own heart energy as it continually unfolds.

Feel the warmth, the sensation, that is beginning to fill your entire chest area.

Continuing to breathe deeply and rhythmically, simply allow the vibration and the power of your own heart to continue to expand until you can feel a great sphere of radiance filling your chest and neck, flowing down through your arms, hands, fingertips, now radiating out through your abdomen and hips, your face and head, encompassing your entire upper body.

Feel the vibration, the sensation, of your heart energy as it continues to unfold in an ever-increasing sphere of active vibration.

Continuing to breathe deeply and rhythmically, simply allow this great sphere of vitality to literally inhabit your entire body.

Notice that you can feel this vitality touching the surface of your skin, and filling the space around you. Stay with this a few moments now.

Now bring your attention to a star, located a hand's length above the top of your head. Notice that you can begin to breathe through this point. As you do, the star begins to vibrate and become more radiant.

Feel the sensation, the vibration, that is beginning to pour down over you as you continue to breathe very deeply and rhythmically through the star above your head.

Feel the sensation of active energy pouring down into your head and across your face, and flowing down through every cell of your body as you give yourself permission to bathe in your own radiance.

You may perhaps be experiencing a tingling or a popping in some areas of your body as they become enlivened and you experience your own energy in new ways. Notice that you may simply allow the power of your awareness and breath to guide the active vibration through any area of your body that seems to have tension or a lack of increased sensation. You may simply allow your own increased vitality to flow easily and smoothly throughout every cell of your entire body. Simply allow yourself to experience your own energy as active vibration and sensation throughout your entire body.

Notice now what you are feeling around you. Notice the sense of something active and vital filling the entire room and surrounding and filling everyone in this core community.

Bring your awareness now to a point at the back of the skull, where the brain and the spinal column meet. Simply place your attention on this point and take about fifteen minutes to meditate and to fully experience yourself filled and surrounded by the sensation of active lifeforce energy.

CHAPTER 4

INTEGRATING AS COMMUNITY

As we work together and fully honor each other, we will call upon the highest creative energy in each of us and create a new sense of community.

A core community, like any community, can be seen basically as a ring of energy. An effective community is a complete ring of energy, one complete flow of a circuit of power. You will have an opportunity to experience yourself as an active participant in such a ring of energy, if you choose, through the group process for this chapter. This is a fundamental process of linking which will be necessary for your core community before you begin any session of group transformative work. The linking of individuals into the core community, and then the linking of the core communities into the core community network builds a vehicle for the Cosmic Christ and makes sweeping global transformation possible through group consciousness.

By creating a chain of communities, interlocking rings of light all across the planet, interlocking rings of consciousness, all communities will be uplifted. Here we are not simply referring to the core community network. The core communities comprise many of these rings of light. But the communities of the entire world community must be united so that if our planet is viewed from above, it would appear to be covered with interlocking webs of conscious energy. That is why it is so important as a core community to begin to link with the animal world, the plant world, and what you consider to be inert matter, as well as other human communities of consciousness. The more communities you are able to interlock with for the sake of the mutual benefit of you, your core community, and all the communities of our universe, the greater results you will be able to generate. The entire planet is becoming Christed.

You must be alert and responsible when you work in community situations because the power generated is not necessarily automatically directed toward the benefit of the entire world community. It is possible to create a community of enormous power that is simply aimed at fulfilling that particular individual community. Our history is full of examples of such communities. The power of the core community network has the potential to create sweeping global change, and the purpose of creating these changes is the transformation of consciousness, the generation of a new experience of identity as Christ for the entire planet and for all the creatures who are associated with the planet.

YOU ARE A CELL IN THE BODY OF EARTH.

To live on this planet is to live within the force field of an enormous conscious being. Knowing this, you can understand that you are a part of the planetary community. You may think of yourself as a cell in the body of the planet. You yourself are an extension of planetary consciousness. As you align your consciousness more directly with an awareness of the planet, you will be more able to transform as the planet changes.

Begin to relax now and find an easy, natural pattern of deep, rhythmic breathing. Simply allow yourself to begin to receive from the planet.

Turn your attention inward to a point at the base of the spine, and very easily and gently begin to breathe through this point.

Notice the vibration as sensation that begins to be activated here. Take a few moments now to develop this experience.

At the base of the spine there is a point where you are able to integrate the energy of the planet. Here, at the base of your spine, you are able to integrate general planetary awareness into individual consciousness as you draw awareness in energy form, consciousness as power, up from the Earth. You have always been doing this, but as you focus your attention on it, you may learn to align yourself more efficiently with the planetary community.

Breathe deeply, and with the power of your breath and your attention, energize this power point at the base of your spine.

Each time you inhale, inhale up through the base of your spine. Inhale more energy from the Earth, up through the base of your spine. Draw it up, and feel the power and the awareness of the planet beginning to fill you.

Notice that as you are inhaling the energy of the planet, you can experience the awareness of the planet.

AT THE BASE OF YOUR SPINE,
YOU MAY INTEGRATE THE AWARENESS OF EARTH.

Just as a mother nurses a child, allow yourself to be nursed by the planet up through the base of your spine. Allow yourself to experience the awareness and the power of the planet as it flows into your body.

Notice the sensation of the flow of energy as it arrives from the planet. Notice where it goes and what it does in your body. Stay with this a few moments as you continue to breathe through the point at the base of your spine.

As you continue to draw the higher vibration of the planetary energy into your body, become aware now of the shift in your own awareness.

If you are able to clearly draw this energy into you, you may, perhaps, have a surprising clarity of focus as you feel the presence of planetary energy inside your body. Simply notice what you are aware of.

If you are able to refer at all times to the awareness of the planet, you will be able at all times to find your place in the process of planetary transformation.

Now become aware of the vibration that you have created in your heart center by drawing this energy of the planet up into you.

In the center of your heart you will find the degree of the strength of your connection with the planet. It is important that you create a truly compassionate relationship with the planet in your heart if you wish to integrate your consciousness more fully with the planet.

Focus your attention in your heart center and begin to breathe through this area. As you do, notice how the vibration here begins to become active and lively.

As you continue to breathe through the center of your heart, allow the energy here to grow, intensify, and radiate. Stay with this experience a few moments.

Feel the power and the awareness of the planet in the center of your heart.

IN THE CENTER OF YOUR HEART,
YOU WILL KNOW YOUR CONNECTION WITH THE PLANET.

If you are truly open to the planet and willing to accept the support of the planet, you will understand and anticipate more clearly the changes to come. This will give you an alertness and a power in the activities of your life. It will give you an opportunity to fulfill your own personal purpose through the changes to come.

Now become aware of the point of consciousness at the top of your spine, where the spine integrates with the brain. Notice what you are experiencing at this point of emerging community consciousness.

Begin to breathe through this point, where the spine integrates with the brain at the back of the skull. Allow the energy to be amplified and clarified through the power of your attention and your breath. Take a few moments to develop this experience.

Feel the power and the awareness of the planet moving up through your body to this point, the back of your skull where your brain and spine intersect.

When you succeed in amplifying and clarifying the energy at the back of the brain at this point, you will gain even greater clarity of self, a certain expansive sense of self. When you bring the planetary energy this far up into you, you may perhaps experience the density of the planet, but you will also experience the expansive awareness of the planet.

Simply allow the energy at the back of the skull to flow downward through the spinal column into the base of the spine and into the Earth. Feel as you integrate your consciousness with the planet inside the planet. Stay with this experience as long as you like.

You may, if you choose, practice consciously aligning with the planet as you walk, especially in nature. As you inhale, simply feel the power and the awareness of the planet moving up through the base of your spine to your heart. As you exhale, feel the combined planetary energy and your awareness flowing from your heart down to the base of your spine and down deep into the planet. Continue this circuit with your breath, and you will find that aligning with the planet in this way can renew and revive you.

Once you have established a conscious linkage, or circuit of connection, with the planet, you may begin to consciously connect with others through the planetary consciousness. This is the first step in consciously integrating as a community, a complete circuit as a ring of energy.

YOU CAN CONNECT
WITH ANYONE OR ANYTHING
THROUGH THE PLANETARY AWARENESS.

Bring your attention once more to your breath now. As you breathe in, notice that you can feel the power and the awareness of the planet moving up into you through the point of power at the base of your spine. Allow it to move up into you and to fill and energize your entire body. Notice the vibration in your heart.

Now, as you exhale, feel the flow of energy as it moves from your heart down to the base of your spine and down deep into the planet.

As you inhale, simply allow the circuit to begin to repeat. As you exhale, allow the circuit to complete.

Feel the circuit of power which continually flows through your connection with the planet as you inhale and exhale. Notice what an easy, natural, and pleasurable process this is. Stay with this experience a few moments.

As you feel the circuit flowing through your heart, bring into your awareness the image or sense of presence of one other member of your core community. Now, as you feel the circuit of energy in your heart, allow it to flow out through your heart to the heart of this other person. With your awareness, witness and feel as the circuit continues to flow down through this other person, down through the heart to the base of the spine, and down deep into the planet. As you inhale, feel once again the circuit as it continually flows up through you to your heart; as you exhale, feel as it flows through your heart to the heart of the other core community member and down deep into the planet. With your deep, steady breathing, simply witness and feel the flow of connection between yourself and this one other member of your core community.

CONNECTING WITH OTHERS THROUGH THE PLANETARY AWARENESS HEALS RELATIONSHIPS.

You may practice this simple but powerful technique of connecting with anyone or anything through the clear awareness of the planetary consciousness with anyone with whom you desire to strengthen or heal a relationship. One of the advantages of this form of healing relationships is that it may be initiated entirely by yourself on an inner level; it is not necessary for the other person to be present or to even consciously know of your healing work. Practicing this simple process with members of your family, household, or workplace can have a very beneficial effect. And more than that, you can also practice aligning with anyone that you consider to be an enemy. As you do, you may be very pleasantly surprised by the results that you generate in the quality of your relationships as you begin to integrate with others through the awareness and the power of the planetary consciousness.

Turn your attention inward upon yourself once again now. Feel your circuit of connection with the planet. Now take as long as you like and consciously integrate with each member of your core community. Take at least a few minutes with each person individually to fully connect and experience your integration through the planetary consciousness. This will be a preparation for the group process of integrating as a community fully aligned with the new consciousness that is emerging in the planetary awareness.

Group Process 4: Aligning as Community

This chapter marks the beginning of the regular session format of (1) community alignment, (2) sharing, (3) process, and (4) celebration.

1. Community Alignment. *The first process provided here is the basic one of aligning as community, the essentials of which you will use to initiate every group session:*

Take a few deep breaths now, and begin to allow the thoughts and the tensions of the day to pass.

Relax, and begin to establish a pattern of deep, rhythmic breathing.

Bring your awareness to your heart now. Begin to very gently and easily breathe through the center of your heart. As you do, feel the sensation, the vibration, that begins to become active.

Take a few moments now to activate the energy of your heart through the power of your breath and your awareness. Allow the sensation of active vibration in your heart to expand and fill your body.

Now become aware of a point of sensation at the base of your spine.

Begin to activate this point through the power of your awareness and your breath. Feel the sensation here as you focus on the base of your spine.

Each time you inhale, inhale up through the point at the base of the spine. Feel the power and the awareness of the planet flowing up into you through this point. Stay with this a few moments now.

Notice the increased vitality you are experiencing throughout your body as the awareness and the power of the planet continue to flow into you.

Feel your connection to the planet.

Become aware now of the sensation in your heart as you sense the planetary energy here.

Inhale the planetary awareness up through the base of your spine to your heart, and allow it to flow back through the heart and down deep into the planet as you exhale. Feel this circuit of connection with the planet with each cycle of inhaling and exhaling. Stay with this experience a few moments now to fully experience this circuit as active power.

Now as you feel the planetary energy in your heart, allow it to stream forth as rays of light from your heart to the heart of each person here in this community.

Feel what it is to be connected through the planetary awareness with each person here.

As you continue to breathe deeply and rhythmically, feel the circuit of planetary energy as it continues to flow up through the base of your spine to your heart and out through your heart to the hearts of all community members here, and down deep into the planet. Simply allow the circuit to naturally continue with your breath.

Feel as you receive the power of the planet through your heart from all others here.

Notice the sensations that you are experiencing throughout your body. Feel your connection with the person to your right. . . the person to your left. Notice that you can follow the flow of energy out from your right from heart to heart, person to person, around the circle of our community.

Now become aware that our core community is a ring of light. Feel what it is to be a member of this community.

Notice now that you can begin to sense the presence of other communities of light.

Now, in the middle of the circle of our community, visualize a radiant sphere of golden light.

As you visualize this sphere of golden light, charge it with the planetary awareness and your personal awareness. Simply create a circuit of energy from the planet up through the base of your spine to your heart and flowing through your heart to the radiant golden sphere, and then down deep into the planet. Notice that you can easily sustain this circuit.

Notice how you are becoming empowered and vitalized through this process.

Now invite all communities of light to join with us, to begin to fill the radiant golden sphere. Feel the shift in the energy of the room as we become aware of an enormous presence. Feel the intensifying presence and power as we are all being united through the planetary consciousness.

Feel the increase in awareness and power. Feel the vitality flowing through your heart and connecting with the hearts of all others as the great radiant sphere begins to expand, and glow, and embrace our community. Feel the awareness and the vitality of an extended community empowering our core community. Now bring your awareness to the point at the back of your skull where your brain and spinal column meet. Stay with this as long as you like.

2. Sharing. *Take some time now for sharing any experiences you may have had during the week as you played with the materials in chapter four of the text.*

3. Process. *The process by which your core community aligned with the entire core community network is one that may be used to align with any community of any size or nature. You may use this same process to align with any community that you wish to neutralize as an enemy, any other parts of the world community, or any community from which you wish to learn:*

Turn your attention inward once again, and establish a pattern of deep, rhythmic breathing. Take a few moments now to consciously strengthen your circuit of connection with the planet and everyone in this core community.

Now take a few moments more and feel our core community as a ring of light. Feel the vitality of the entire core community network, the extended community, flowing through your heart and the hearts of all in this community.

Begin now to visualize a sphere of light in the center of our community. Charge this light sphere with the planetary awareness and your personal awareness as you consciously create a circuit of active energy up from the planet through the base of your spine to your heart and out to the sphere of light and down deep into the planet. Keep this circuit vitalized through the power of your awareness and your deep, rhythmic breathing.

Now, let us begin to align with the other members of the world community. Invite the entire animal community to join with us. Feel the shift in the room as the energy of this visiting community begins to fill the sphere of light in the center of our community.

Now simply allow the sphere of this visiting community to expand until it is as big as the ring of our community. Notice what you are feeling at the back of your skull where the brain and the spinal column meet.

Understand that as you link up with any community, you may learn from it on a telepathic level. This telepathy may be experienced as thoughts or images, vibrations, or sensations in any part of your body.

Feel what it is for our core community to compassionately link its heart energy with the animal community. Stay with this a few moments.

Now allow the visiting community to be released; allow the energy to return to its rightful place in the planetary consciousness.

Understand that once having made this link, you may always bring it back. If you wish, you may repeat this process of consciously integrating as community to align with the other major communities in the world community: the plant and the mineral communities.

4. Celebration!

CHAPTER 5

EXPERIENCING CONTINUOUS CONSCIOUSNESS

CONSCIOUSNESS is always unfolding. In the development of human consciousness, different parts of the brain have developed simultaneously with different levels of consciousness. The evolution of human consciousness has gone through several stages from the point of initial development in the area of the lower back half of the brain.

At this time, the current level of development of personal identity tends, generally, to be focused in the front part of the brain. In other times of human history, other parts of the brain have been the primary functional units and motivators of activity. Now the entire human brain is functional.

At this time, the cycle may be seen as completing and returning back to a level of personal consciousness. Now that individuality has been developed, community consciousness is again unfolding. This consciousness focuses in the lower back part of the brain where the brain intersects with the spinal column. Within this area, there is the focus of deeper instinctual awareness and community awareness.

This area was active a long time ago. In this area at one time, the group consciousness of human ancestors was predominant. Telepathic communication was the predominant form of communication. Awareness tended to function on group levels. All members of the society had access to the total awareness of the group.

This currently unfolding awareness will be different as a result of evolution from the way it functioned last time. Now the individual will be integrated into the world community through this process of evolution. Individuality will not be lost. Individuality, however, will gain a great deal more fulfillment because the individual experiences greatest satisfaction when it loses the sense of separation from the rest of the world.

EVEN ENLIGHTENMENT
CAN BE SHARED BY A COMMUNITY
THAT IS IN RESONANCE.

The potential of the unfolding community consciousness is truly awesome. Even the possibility of enlightenment can be shared in a community of individuals who are in telepathic resonance with each other.

In the community, should one member of the community achieve a state of awareness such as enlightenment, the entire community connected through the consciousness in the lower back part of the brain where it integrates with the spinal column will be able to share in this experience of enlightenment. All the members would not automatically experience enlightenment, for they each would need to find their own individual attunement to that level of awareness in present time and place. But they each would have an opportunity to find resonance that would inspire that awareness within themselves. Even in a community of enlightened individuals, individuality will be maintained. Individuality is part of human nature.

These states are a natural resource of human consciousness that have been available for a great deal of time. There are those that you know of in past times who have achieved these states. But these states of consciousness will now be more readily accessible. Humankind in its historic evolution has done a great deal to make these states of consciousness more and more accessible through the experience of community.

For example, all of our processes of communication today ultimately are interweaving with the human group consciousness. The radio waves, television waves, microwaves, and so on, that are being used for communication and energy generation are being intercepted by the human group consciousness. They are becoming part of human consciousness.

At this time, most people are incapable of thinking without intercepting energy vibrations of certain communications broadcasts. They are being interwoven into their thought patterns. While you do not have receivers in your brain, typically, to interpret those patterns the way radios, televisions, and radar systems interpret them, nevertheless, you are processing a great deal of human-produced raw energy of communication.

These levels of broadcast information are often useful for the development of your consciousness, regardless of the intent of those who broadcast a radio or television show or the material contained in the intended broadcast. The energy itself is generating a familiarity with certain levels of consciousness. The broadcasts being generated are often functioning at levels of energy vibration that are directly affecting the planetary field of consciousness. They are helping to raise the vibration of the entire planetary field.

Human consciousness is part of the pattern of planetary consciousness. You, as an individual unit of the human consciousness, function as what may be called a cellular member of the planetary consciousness. What you do and the way you do it directly affects the total planetary consciousness. It does not matter what you do and do not do; you are directly affecting that consciousness.

YOU GENERATE CONSCIOUSNESS, NOT SIMPLY RECEIVE IT.

Your thoughts also broadcast at frequencies. Your thoughts directly pattern the physical, emotional, mental, and spiritual experiences of your individual identity. They tend to create these patterns of individual identity, and these patterns are active in planetary processes.

The entire planetary consciousness field consisting of planet, atmosphere, and energy aura is generating internally and externally higher vibrations of energy for the time of a new reality. Communication processes contribute to this increase in vibration, but your own internal consciousness development also helps to generate this level of consciousness. It is a basic function of human identity to generate consciousness, not simply to receive it.

Focus your attention inward now upon your own conscious experience of yourself at this time. Allow yourself to be comfortable and to find a pattern of deep breathing that supports your experience of relaxation and comfort.

Focus first upon an area just above and behind your eyes, the area of the lower half of the front half of the brain. Simply become aware as clearly as you can of the experience of energy as perception and sensation in the lower half of the front half of the brain. Notice what you are experiencing here.

REFINE THE CONSCIOUSNESS
IN YOUR FRONT BRAIN
TO EXPERIENCE THE NEWLY AVAILABLE ENERGIES.

Notice that in this area of the brain there is a dominant vibration and various reciprocal vibrations. You do not need to seek out these vibratory experiences. You may simply allow yourself to be aware that they are here.

Notice that you experience these vibrations from the part of the brain that you are observing. This part of the brain is witnessing its own experience. It is here, in the lower half of the front half of the brain, that you experience directly the functions of this area of the brain.

Take a moment now, and without strain or effort, allow the vibratory sensations you are experiencing in the lower half of the front half of your brain to become stronger and clearer simply by breathing through this area and paying attention. Simply allow the rebalancing and retuning of your consciousness. Notice what an easy and pleasurable experience this is as you follow the development of your own consciousness now for a few moments.

Notice now how your perception has changed. Become aware of the shift in your self-awareness as well as your awareness of the environment around you.

Notice the way in which your thoughts flow through this area of your brain. Feel the continuity of your thoughts in this area of the brain. You do not need to analyze this experience and to understand with your rational mind. Simply feel the sensations. The next levels of human consciousness development will be experienced first largely as sensation, not idea.

Become aware that you can sense the interrelationship of the individual thoughts in this area. This experience of individual thoughts finding continuity—a common resonant vibration in an entire area of the brain experienced as sensation—is directly correlated to the experience that you can have connecting with others in community.

Continuing to breathe deeply, allow your awareness now to focus upon the upper half of the front half of the brain. Notice the vibratory patterns that are active in this area. Notice the predominant vibratory tone of consciousness.

Very gently and easily begin to breathe through the area of the upper half of the front half of the brain.

Notice what you directly experience in the upper half of the front half of your brain as you now refocus and retune the energy in this part of the brain. Be aware that you do not need to try to do this; you may simply allow and witness.

Become aware now that you can sense a primary tone of total brain function at this time. Notice that a level of awareness that is instantly familiar to you, and yet seems different than your normal state of awareness is activated.

YOU HAVE
A DOMINANT VIBRATORY TONE OF CONSCIOUSNESS
IN YOUR FRONT BRAIN.

From this retuned consciousness you are able to experience a broader and far more profound perception of the world around you. The renewal of active awareness in the lower back half of the brain would not be productive if a process of external perception and individual evaluation in the front half of the brain were to atrophy. If you wish to generate an accelerated experience of this newly available community consciousness within your own mind, you must synthesize your consciousness in the front of your brain and raise it to higher, more clear, more powerful vibrations so that your consciousness may remain in a creatively effective balance.

Very gently, and with a soft focus of attention, begin to breathe through the entire front half of the brain. Feel as the upper and the lower halves of the front half of the brain become more profoundly attuned.

Notice that you are beginning to sense the dominant vibratory tone of consciousness in the entire front half of the brain. You can perceive more clearly the interrelationship of all the thoughts that are being processed through the entire front half of the brain in relation to the dominant tone. Notice that this is a sensory experience. You may simply allow your rational mind to rest and to witness. Take a few moments now to continue to breathe through the entire front half of your brain. Simply accept and appreciate your experience of retuning your consciousness.

YOUR ABILITY TO FOCUS IN THE FRONT BRAIN IS RELATED TO YOUR ABILITY TO REFOCUS YOUR IDENTITY PATTERNS.

The typical function of thought in our society at this time in history tends to be periodic consciousness, consciousness generated in regular and irregular intervals. This has had its creative purpose in human development, but it can be evolved. This level of evolution is accessible to you in your natural brain function.

As you experience the attunement of the entire front half of the brain, you are now able to more clearly focus upon your fulfillment. It is through your ability to focus your awareness in this area of the brain that you are able to refocus your identity patterns. This re-creating of personal identity patterns to those of greater personal fulfillment is a crucial step in the development of planetary consciousness. On the most fundamental level, personal transformation is planetary transformation; you are a unit of planetary consciousness.

The planet itself generates a great diversity of land masses and bodies of water, types of weather and climates. You are no different. You have a variety of thoughts and experiences, and you have many different patterns within your identity. This allows you great creativity. But you have a continuous awareness that unites them all. All the patterns of your identity are unified in a greater picture of consciousness.

Focus once more upon the area of the front half of the brain. As you do, consider what it feels like to be fully satisfied.

Focus upon a point approximately in the center of the front half of the brain, a point midway between the center of the head and the front of the head. Very gently amplify the sensation and vibration here through the power of your breath and your awareness. As you do, focus upon what it feels like to be satisfied.

Become aware of your capacity to generate continuous consciousness of this experience. Then, rather than referring to the experience of satisfaction in periodic bursts of attention, you may be aware of it as a continuous state, a state that can be interwoven through the varieties of your experience in the world.

YOU ARE ALWAYS
AN ACTIVE INFLUENCE
UPON CONSCIOUSNESS.

Consider who you must be to have the capacity to generate this level of self-awareness. Do not judge the degree of effectiveness of the apparent results that you have been able to create in this exercise. It is not the image of your own satisfaction and experience that is primary. It is the experience of this process itself. You are able to turn your attention towards the issue of satisfaction. Whether or not you feel you have created it in your life, you are able to generate the resonance of your potential thoughtform within yourself, your environment, and the planetary consciousness.

You are always an active influence upon the total consciousness of several planes of existence simultaneously. It is not necessary that you comprehend all of these levels of consciousness. It is only important that you are able to accept and appreciate your own creative role, and that you understand that consciousness does not develop; it simply unfolds and expands. Consciousness is already whole, complete.

When you experience this fact, you will realize that you do not need to break-down your apparent limitations. Your truly unlimited consciousness floats through forms. It generates forms as energy patterns, not as rigid structures. Consider this, and you will appreciate the use of continuous consciousness.

Now that you have developed the initial experience of this

level of consciously generated consciousness, you may attune this consciousness to your physical experience so that you will be able to use it.

Focus your attention on the base of your spine. As you do, notice that there is a harmony here with the energy patterns in the front half of your brain. As you focus upon this resonance at the base of your spine, notice the point seems to become magnetic. You may simply allow harmonious energy patterns from the front of your brain to flow down into the base of your spine, the point of physical power. Take a moment to fully experience this alignment.

Notice the shift in your experience as the consciousness at the front half of your brain is harmonized with that at the base of your spine. Simply be aware of the sensations at the base of your spine.

Become aware, at the base of your spine, of a relationship, a resonant harmony, with the vibratory awareness of the planet in the area that is below your feet. Feel the natural process of attunement to the planetary consciousness in the Earth itself. Feel the harmony of an energy alignment from the base of your spine deep into the Earth. Take as long as you like now to enjoy this experience.

CONSCIOUSNESS
DOES NOT DEVELOP;
IT SIMPLY EXPANDS.

This process has been an experience of developing continuous consciousness through the front brain. Through the group process for this chapter, you will have an opportunity to expand upon this experience to unfold continuous consciousness at the point of community awareness in the lower back part of the brain.

CONSCIOUSNESS IS ALWAYS WHOLE.

The process of developing continuous consciousness is a natural one. It is already within the range of your skills. You have already proven your capability to generate enormous levels of consciousness experience. Consider the degree of transformative work that was accomplished from the moment you initiated conception to the moment of your birth. Consider the enormous transformative process that you generated from the moment of birth to the time of adolescence. Consider all the cycles that have proceeded since then. You are extremely experienced already in the development of conscious experience. In the community environment, you simply have the opportunity to share the joy and the adventure of the next stage of human development.

CONTINUOUS CONSCIOUSNESS
IS
NATURAL TO YOU.

Group Process 5: Experiencing Continuous Consciousness

Before you use the process presented here, remember to align as a community and then to share your experiences of the week related to your play with chapter five.

Turn your attention inward now, and begin to establish a pattern of deep, rhythmic breathing.

Notice that you can breathe through your entire body simultaneously. As you do, you begin to feel a sense of great expansiveness.

Take a few moments now to fully develop this experience.

Now bring your awareness to a point in the center of the front half of your brain, a point midway between the center of your head and the front of your head. Very gently and easily, begin to activate this point by breathing through it.

Notice the sensation, the vibration, that you are experiencing here in the center of the front half of your brain.

Now bring your awareness to a point at the lower back of your skull, where the brain and the spinal column meet.

Notice what you feel here.

As you breathe in now, inhale from this point in the back of your skull.

Notice that you can feel active sensation flowing from the front half of your brain to the point where the brain and the spinal column meet as you continue to breathe deeply and rhythmically through this point at the back of the skull.

Stay with this experience for a few minutes to fully develop it.

Notice now the vibration, the sensation, that you are experiencing here, at the point where the brain and the spinal column meet.

As you continue to focus on this point of emerging community consciousness, become aware that you can sense the active awareness of all others in our core community.

Continuing to breathe deeply and rhythmically, notice that you can feel an active awareness flowing through you, surrounding you, filling the circle of the community. Stay with this awhile.

Become aware now of what you are experiencing in your heart.

As you continue to focus on the point at the back of your skull where your brain and spinal column intersect, notice that you can simultaneously feel an active awareness flowing through your heart.

Notice that you can feel your connection with the entire world community in your heart.

Continuing to breathe deeply and rhythmically, stay with this experience a few moments.

Notice what you are feeling throughout your body now.

Notice the joy and the satisfaction that you are experiencing.

Now bring your awareness once again to the point in the center of the front brain. As you do, simply be aware of your joy and satisfaction.

Feel your satisfaction resonating, here at the point in the center of the front half of your brain.

Feel your satisfaction resonating in your heart.

Feel satisfaction and joy resonating in the active awareness that fills you, that surrounds you, that seems to flow through you and your core community and the entire world community.

Stay with this a few moments and give yourself permission to experience fully.

Notice now that you can feel the resonance of your joy and your satisfaction at the base of your spine and, simultaneously, deep in the planet.

Now bring your awareness once again to the point at the back of your skull where the brain and the spinal column meet. Feel the sensation of active continuous consciousness as you meditate on this point for the next ten minutes.

CHAPTER 6

DEVELOPING PRESENCE

YOUR presence is your expression of Spirit. Presence is the awareness and expression of Spirit, that energy which binds together everything in the universe. As you develop presence, you will generate transformation that will endure and further your life and the lives of those around you.

Without a sense of presence, it will be difficult for you to be sure that your transformative work is appropriate to your well-being. To understand well-being, understand that there is always being. Everything knows itself in its deeper consciousness, and this is being. Well-being is simply a clarity of that consciousness, that sense of purpose. With well-being, you are aware that your personality is actually an extension of your deep self, that part of you that is timeless, eternal, infinite, that knows its own purpose.

Your personality is a means to express your deepest potentials, but first you must have a sense of well-being. You must have presence, the awareness of yourself as an energy being that expresses through a personality. Unless you have that awareness, you will not be able to clearly perceive the purpose of your deep self.

When you have presence, your personality is an active representative of your deepest potentials. You may understand this with a simple metaphor. Consider a tree growing from the planet into the sky. The tree knows itself as a tree, and yet it also knows itself as a representative of the potentials of the planet from which it grows. It sees itself as an opportunity to extend the power of the planet out into the atmosphere. Your personality is like a tree extending from the planet of your own deeper consciousness. You will have presence to the degree that your personality is rooted in your deeper consciousness. Then you will generate transformation that is powerful and effective for yourself and the world.

YOUR PRESENCE
IS
YOUR EXPRESSION OF SPIRIT.

So that you may more fully understand and experience presence, turn your attention in upon yourself now. Begin to breathe deeply with ease. Allow yourself to relax and be comfortable.

Now bring your attention to the area of your heart. As you continue to breathe very easily and deeply, focus on the bottom half of your heart center.

Notice that you can begin to breathe through this point in the bottom half of your heart center. Take a few moments for this experience.

Feel the energy here in the bottom half of your heart center becoming active as you breathe through this area. Feel the vibration that begins to grow.

Feel the physical sensation of active vibration originating from the bottom half of your heart center. As you continue to breathe through this point, feel the way this vibration—perhaps as waves, perhaps as beams of energy—radiates outward from the bottom half of your heart center into the top half of the heart and into the chest area, and out into the shoulders, and down into the abdomen.

Allow yourself to experience this natural and pleasurable sensation radiating out from the bottom of your heart. Notice how easy this is. You do not have to force. You may simply allow this energy to flow, to expand, to increase, and to clarify as you breathe through the point in the bottom half of your heart center.

Become aware that you have raised the vibration here through the power of your breath and your will. Follow the sensation as it is awakened, amplified, clarified, and cleansed in the bottom half of the heart center.

Notice that from this point in the bottom half of your heart center, you can begin to move deeper and ever deeper into yourself. Follow this sensation and flow of energy as it seems to flow inward now.

Notice that you are beginning to move into a realm of self-awareness that seems to lie underneath your personality, a realm of awareness that lies beneath your sense of yourself in this lifetime.

Feel yourself following the flow of energy in the bottom half of your heart center which flows inward. Feel yourself now reaching closer and closer to a point deep within you of harmonizing energy to which you can relate the energy from the lower half of the heart center.

Feel a bridge of energy extending between your deep self and the lower half of your heart center.

PRESENCE
BRIDGES YOUR DEEPER AWARENESS
WITH PRESENT-TIME EXPERIENCE.

Feel the flow of energy radiating out from within your deep self to the lower half of your heart center. Notice the sensation. Feel the power moving through you that flows as waves of sensation from deep within you, from that part of you that is not dependent upon the circumstances of your present lifetime. Stay with this awhile.

Notice that you can feel your personal identity as being more like the tree that grows from the planet of your deep self. Feel your present-time, present-place identity as a creative opportunity to reach out with the best that is within you.

Feel the vibration and the physical sensation of the wisdom of your deep self within you radiating outward. Feel it as simply presence.

Your presence bridges your deeper awareness with present-time experience so that you may use the greatest potential within you. This will generate transformation that is appropriate to the changes of experience that you and all others will have in this time of transformation, rather than to what you perceive as your needs or the world's needs.

Again, the presence that you initiate at the most profound level available to you at any time is the experience of Spirit. Spirit is within you. When individuals are joined together in a community through the mutual awareness of that presence of Spirit within each one, the capabilities to use Spirit are extended for all.

Presence can be invoked from the Spirit force within you and around you. And more than that, you can live in presence. You do not need to simply invoke presence, but you can live in presence.

Presence can be a significant factor in healing. Presence is most powerful in working with another when you create a complete relationship. All complete relationships are fundamentally a factor of three. A relationship on its most fundamental level involves two individuals and the aura of the relationship that binds them together, the mutual awareness that is created by the interaction of the two individuals. This always creates a third level of awareness, which may be shared presence.

A fundamental electromagnetic relationship of energy is based on this same principle. There are the two poles of negative and positive, and the third identity that is created by their relationship, the circuit of energy that flows through the poles and binds them together.

The aura of the relationship can be shared presence. You can create this on a subtle level if your sense of personal presence is so strong that you awaken presence within the other in the relationship. This is an act of healing. It is establishing a relationship of Spirit to Spirit.

THE AURA OF A RELATIONSHIP
CAN BE SHARED PRESENCE.

If you can establish a direct experience of presence within yourself, and you wish to promote healing within another, let the Spirit within you be strong in your heart center first, and then throughout the rest of your identity that can sustain it. You may then call upon and perhaps awaken the presence in the other. If the other feels that presence, you will generate the most powerful healing that is appropriate at that time.

Presence can always be awakened in the area of a problem if

you are able to reach deeply enough. You can use any problem or challenge to reach presence. If presence is to be awakened, it may be awakened in the area of the challenge, in the area of the heart, in the area of the deep abdomen, and in the area of the center of the head. Presence is an experience; it is not simply concept.

PRESENCE MAY BE AWAKENED
IN THE HEART, DEEP ABDOMEN, CENTER OF THE HEAD,
AND AREA OF ANY "PROBLEM."

Focus in upon yourself once more. Place your full attention on your heart center. Begin to breathe with ease through this area. Stay with this awhile.

Simply become aware of your experience and your sensations on any level. If they seem to be normal experiences, do not feel that you are doing anything wrong. What is natural can be healthy. What you experience, though it may seem an ordinary experience, can be a sign of well-being just as an intense experience of this energy at this time may be natural and may serve you. It is important that you simply be aware of the power of your own energy, and your perception and experience of it.

Become aware now of the sensation, the perception of energy, here at the very center of your heart. Allow this energy to increase and clarify through the power of your breath and your will. Allow this energy to grow, to vibrate more strongly, and to radiate itself more clearly.

Allow the entire heart center now to be filled with this energy.

Notice that from deep within your heart, you can feel the wisdom and the power of your deep self radiating up and out through your heart.

You can feel your presence. Stay with this experience awhile. Experience it in whatever way you can at this time, and do not judge your experience. Your appreciation and acceptance of your presence, at whatever level is appropriate to you at this time, will activate and awaken your presence further.

Judgment is not evaluation of process. Judgment is a distraction from the essentials. It is important that you remain focused upon essentials if you wish to fully experience presence.

Stay with your experience of presence in your heart for a few moments.

Now become aware of a point in your deep abdomen that is beginning to become active and to resonate with your heart.

Very gently, begin to deeply breathe through this resonant point in your deep abdomen.

Notice the increased vibration and sensation in the area of your deep abdomen as you activate this area through the power of your breath and your will. Stay with this a moment.

Feel the energy that flows between these two points, the area of your deep abdomen and your heart. Feel how they seem to vibrate in harmony.

Notice that you can begin to feel presence in your deep abdomen.

Now bring your attention to a point slightly above the middle of your head that is beginning to vibrate with increased sensation. Begin to activiate this area further through your breath and attention.

Notice that you can feel presence here, near the center of your head.

Notice that you can simultaneously feel presence at the center of your head, the deep abdomen, and the heart. Feel how these three points seem to vibrate in harmony with one another. Feel the flow of energy between these three points. Stay with this a moment.

Become aware that you are beginning to feel that part of you that exists beyond time, that is always vital, always active and self-aware, radiating out through these three points simultaneously.

Notice that you can simply allow this radiance and power, presence, to radiate through all the cells of your body. Allow presence to fill your entire body now.

Allow presence to fill your entire body and the area around you. Feel presence in and around you. Stay with this experience for as long as you like, and feel the shift in your awareness.

In all your transformative work, identify presence. Feel it in yourself first, and then you will be able to assist the activation of presence in others and in your environment. Through your presence, you will be able to generate transformation that will effectively touch others and your world.

Presence is a bridge between the self that is not aware of itself and the self that is fully aware. With presence, you actively radiate the timeless and eternal wisdom that is within you, that Christ consciousness, into present time and place.

WITH PRESENCE
YOU ACTIVELY RADIATE THE COSMIC CHRIST
INTO PRESENT TIME AND PLACE.

Group Process 6: Developing Presence

Turn your attention inward now and begin to establish a pattern of deep, rhythmic breathing.

Now bring your awareness to a point in the bottom half of your heart center. Begin to very gently and easily breathe through this point.

Notice the vibration, the sensation, that begins to grow, here in the bottom half of your heart as you very deeply and rhythmically breathe through this point.

Feel this sensation as a sphere of energy that continually expands. Take a few moments to go deeply into this experience.

Notice that you can feel the increased vibration, sensation, throughout your entire body now.

Simply feel the vibration as active power rippling out from your heart through your chest, arms, neck, abdomen, head, legs, hands and fingertips, into the space around you.

Now as you feel the active power flowing in your heart, notice that you can feel it flowing inward. Begin to follow the flow of vitality that seems to flow inward, that seems to flow into the very depths of yourself.

Notice now what you are experiencing as you continue to breathe deeply and rhythmically and to allow your awareness to look inward ever deeper.

Notice that you can begin to sense a timeless awareness. Notice that you are beginning to experience yourself as ageless, as ever-vital, as all-knowing.

Feel now, as you look out from this awareness, how you may witness. Feel how you, as deep self, are unaffected by the circumstances of your world. Feel your clear, vital, awakened awareness.

As you continue to breathe deeply and rhythmically through your heart, allow your deep-self awareness to radiate out from this deep center of focus. Feel the power and the clarity of your awakened awareness flowing out through your heart. Feel your presence.

Now, as you focus upon your presence radiating out through your heart, simultaneously place your awareness on the heart of one other person in this core community.

Simply feel your presence in your heart. Stay with this a moment as you simultaneously focus upon the heart of one other person here.

Notice that you can feel presence in your heart and the heart of the other community member. Feel how your sense of presence is even stronger now.

Take some time now to experience your presence resonating with the presence of each other person in this core community.

Notice what you are experiencing in the room now. Notice the aura of presence that is filling this community and the environment.

Notice that you can feel a reciprocal vibration now in your deep abdomen. Feel your presence in your deep abdomen.

Continuing to breathe deeply and rhythmically, begin to feel the resonance of your presence in your deep abdomen. As you do, simultaneously place your awareness on the point in the deep abdomen of all other community members.

Notice how your presence is growing stronger in your deep abdomen.

Feel what you are experiencing in the center of your head. Notice that you can feel your presence in the center of your head now.

Notice that you can simultaneously feel presence resonating in the head of every community member. Notice that you can feel this presence as a ring of light connecting everyone through the point in the center of the head.

You can feel your presence in the center of your head, in your heart, and in your deep abdomen.

As you continue to breathe deeply and rhythmically, simply allow your presence to begin to inhabit your entire body. Feel your presence resonating in all the cells of your body.

Feel presence resonating through your heart and now, throughout the environment, throughout the entire world community.

Feel what it is to be filled and surrounded by presence, and simultaneously now, focus your awareness at the back of your skull where the brain and the spinal column meet. Stay with this experience as long as you like and at least for the next five minutes.

CHAPTER 7

CLARIFYING YOUR PATH

IN all of your transformative work, you will create what is most beneficial to you if you seek what brings you the greatest clarity of self at any time. Seek clarity rather than the one state that you believe will be the experience of enlightenment. You cannot truly conceive of the state of enlightenment before hand, and it does not serve you to anticipate illusions. That obscures your perception of the reality that is available to you.

Your transformation does not depend upon clarity; you will create transformation whether or not you experience clarity. But expansion of your consciousness as you undergo transformation is produced through clarity. With a sense of clarity, you may learn to realize your identity unfolding. Essentially, clarity is the awareness that you have an individual purpose in a universal context.

Clarity is the state that will empower you in all the activities of your life. As you look into the world with clarity, you will be able to choose the most meaningful path for yourself. Then transformation will not be the process of pain or of violent release; it can simply be the process of self-realization. You can begin to clearly see who you are.

So that you may come to be aware of the channels within yourself to your own personal clarity, focus your attention inward at this time, and begin to breathe deeply, slowly, and rhythmically.

Become aware of your capacity to create a sense of peace within yourself. You cannot have clarity if you do not have a peaceful balance within yourself.

As you look inward, focus on a point inside the center of your abdominal area.

Breathe through this point in the abdominal area. As you do, notice the sensation that begins to become active. Stay with this a few moments.

Be aware of the sensations at a point in your deep abdomen. Be aware of the perceptions that you experience as you activate this energy through the power of your breath and your will.

As you continue to maintain your awareness of the perceptions and sensations that you are experiencing as this energy is activated, notice that at this point in your abdomen, you are able to activate the wisdom of your physical existence.

IN YOUR DEEP ABDOMEN
YOU CAN ACTIVATE YOUR PHYSICAL WISDOM.

The advantage of physical wisdom is that the body is directly aligned with its environment. You do not need to cultivate bodily wisdom; you need only cultivate your awareness, appreciation, and clear communication of your bodily wisdom. If you need a source of arbitration within yourself to decide a simple solution or make a choice between two alternatives, look to the body, to the center of the deep abdomen.

Focus in upon this area, and allow yourself to begin to expand your awareness of your bodily wisdom.

As you continue to breathe through this area inside the center of your abdomen, feel the increase of aware energy. Focus not just on the intensity of vibration, but focus also upon an increased awareness in your deep abdomen.

Feel for yourself what it is to know, in your body, what is appropriate and what is not. The body does not speculate on the potential of the future or the past. The body contains the wisdom to maintain itself in proper relationship to present time and place.

Consider a choice, on any level of your life experience, that you have between two alternatives. Simply consider that choice in your mind.

Feel what you experience in the abdomen. Focus for a few moments on your choice, and feel the body's response to each of these choices.

Simply consider this, and breathe deeply and slowly. Notice what you learn from this exercise.

Notice that while wisdom seems to originate in the abdominal area, nevertheless, the entire physical body is actually experiencing the wisdom. The abdominal area is simply a focal point at which the physical wisdom is expressed more clearly. It is not in itself an isolated brain-like area. The wisdom gathered in the abdomen is the accumulated wisdom throughout the entire body. It is set up in the body's energy field as a polarity to the activity and intensity of the mind.

YOU HAVE ACCESS TO THE WISDOM OF THIS WORLD THROUGH YOUR BODY.

You have access to the wisdom of this world through your body. If you are able to fully open to this level of clarity within yourself, you will find that you are able to truly know your path in this world.

Focus once more on the point in the deep abdomen. Become aware of a sense of certainty that arises within your body. Notice an awareness that does not doubt but is totally aligned with the world in present time and place.

Feel this energy as it begins to grow.

You may use this wisdom to find your most appropriate way in the activities of your life. The path that is most appropriate for you will always be directly beneath your feet if you are able to be continually aware of the wisdom that is contained within your body.

Bring your awareness now to your heart center. Notice what you are experiencing here.

Through the power of your awareness and your breath, begin to activate the energy in your heart center. Feel yourself opening and expanding through the heart area. Stay with this experience a few moments.

Become aware that you can sense your presence.

You can feel your presence becoming active. Notice that as you do, you are beginning to sense the presence of the wisdom of your deep self. Simply allow yourself to experience this as sensation.

Feel the alignment of the wisdom of the deep self with the wisdom of the body.

Be aware now of the sense of purposefulness that is awakening within you at this time.

This sense of purposefulness, your intent, is far more fundamental and important than any sense of purpose that is dependent upon forces that have not actualized in present time and place. Your intent is the motivating purpose of your life; it is the motivating force through which you have created all the experience of your life. This realization that purpose is fundamentally personal intent is the key to clarity.

CLARITY IS THE AWARENESS
THAT YOU HAVE AN INDIVIDUAL PURPOSE
IN A UNIVERSAL CONTEXT.

As you continue to breathe deeply and rhythmically, feel as the intent of your consciousness is more directly focused in alignment with your bodily wisdom. Feel this as sensation, not idea, throughout your entire body. Stay with this a moment.

Now choose one area of your life in which you wish to initiate a transformation into a new, more expanded and satisfying level of experience. Choose an aspect where you have the greatest desire.

As you consider this area of your life, simultaneously feel the sensation of wisdom growing in your abdominal area. Feel the sensation of wisdom growing throughout your entire body.

Notice that you can sense an awareness of the most appropriate path for you that will bring you to transformation in this area of concern in your life. Do not seek an idea; simply, for now, feel this as sensation.

Resolution may appear to you, and you may accept it. But for now, seek the clarity of your path. This will lead you ultimately to a resolution that is appropriate.

Allow the energy from the abdominal area to flow down through the legs, down to the feet. Feel the flow of energy down through your feet to the floor below you and into the planet.

Feel how your wisdom is aligned with the wisdom of the planet.

Notice the awareness that is growing within you that your body is already aware of the purpose, the intent, of the planetary transformation at this time. Feel the awareness that is growing within you of your own path of transformation and the alliance your path has with planetary transformation.

It will be difficult for you to generate transformation in your life at any time if you do not honor the context in which you work. If you are not aligned with the process of planetary transformation, you will find personal growth to be more and more a struggle. The results and satisfaction you experience during a time of transformation are dependent upon your clarity. Again, clarity is the awareness that you have an individual purpose in a universal context.

Feel the focus of profound physical wisdom in your abdominal area.

Draw this energy directly up through the center of your body to the top half of your heart center. Feel what it is to inhale this energy up to your heart.

YOUR ASPIRATIONS ARE CONTAINED IN THE TOP HALF OF YOUR HEART CENTER.

In the top half of your heart center, you will find a great deal of your aspiration, a great deal of the power to satisfy your intent through dedication to the fulfillment of yourself.

Feel this energy as it expresses itself in the top half of your heart center. Feel the radiance of this energy as it seems to ripple its power from the top half of the heart center out through your chest, to the shoulders, to the midsection.

Notice what it is to activate a triangular field of energy whose reference points are the top half of your heart and the points near the tips of your shoulders. Feel the energy flowing in both directions through these three reference points.

Here is the circuit through which you align the aspirations of your consciousness as energy with your capabilities and your wisdom as a physical being. Here you are able to align the best of your intent with the best of your capabilities.

Feel as the energy in the top half of the heart center, the tip of each shoulder, and in the deep abdomen is refocused simply by your direct attention.

Feel what it is to know the best of your intent and the best of your capabilities simultaneously. When you create these two realizations as one simultaneous realization, you cannot help but know your path. To know this is to be in the state of greatest possible clarity for fulfilling your aspiration.

KNOW YOUR PATH
BY ALIGNING YOUR INTENT
WITH YOUR CAPABILITIES.

Feel this triangular field of energy in the upper body aligned with the power point in the abdomen. Continuing to breathe deeply and rhythmically, feel what it is to know your own clarity.

Feel your deeper level of wisdom rising within you as active power rather than concept.

As you continue to generate clearer power through the circuit defined by these four points of reference, bring into your awareness the challenge in your life that is furthest from resolution.

Simply align the challenge itself with the circuit of conscious energy through the body by feeling the circuit of conscious energy in your body and having an image, or a thought, of this challenge. You do not need to seek the information that defines the way that leads you to a resolution of this challenge.

Continue to focus on the energy flowing through the circuit created by these four points, and particularly be aware of the energy contained in the top half of your heart center.

CLARITY IS THE COMBINED
WISDOM OF YOUR DEEP SELF AND
WISDOM OF YOUR BODY.

Become aware now of your presence. Feel the active awareness of your deep self in the top half of your heart center.

Allow the power of your deep self now to further align with and empower the circuit of self-aware energy which originates in the body itself. Stay with this awhile.

Over the next week, you may find the awareness that you need coming to the surface to assist you in creating appropriate resolution of this challenge in your life. If you receive these inspirations during the coming week, claim them as a result of the combined active power of both the wisdom of your deep self and the wisdom of your body. You may appreciate your capacity for clarity.

You yourself are the source of your joy and transformation. You are already the source of your satisfaction. This awareness provides constant clarity on your path.

Group Process 7: Clarifying Your Path

Turn your attention inward now and begin to establish a pattern of deep, rhythmic breathing.

Focus your awareness on the point of body wisdom in the deep abdomen. Begin to activate this point through the power of your awareness and your breath.

Take a few moments to fully develop this experience.

Notice now the active sensation of your body wisdom in your deep abdomen.

As you continue to breathe deeply and rhythmically through the point in your deep abdomen, simultaneously place your awareness on the deep abdomen of one other core community member.

Feel the harmony of vibrations as you resonate from your point of body wisdom with that of another community member.

Feel the vibration, the sensation, in your deep abdomen as it begins to grow stronger.

Become aware now that you are beginning to sense the resonance, the harmonious vibration, of body wisdom in the deep abdomen of all the core community members.

Notice, as you continue to breathe deeply and rhythmically through the point in your deep abdomen, that you can sense body wisdom becoming stronger throughout our entire community. Stay with this a moment and simply notice what you experience.

Feel what it is to be part of this community in present time and present place.

Now bring your awareness to the top half of your heart center. Begin to activate this point through the power of your awareness and your breath.

Take a moment to fully develop this experience.

Feel the vibration, the sensation, as it begins to flow now from the top half of your heart center out through your chest to the tips of your shoulders. Feel as a triangular field of active energy begins to flow in both directions from the top of your heart to the tips of the shoulders.

As you continue to breathe deeply and rhythmically through your heart, notice now that from deep within, you are beginning to feel your presence.

Feel your presence becoming active and infusing the energy pattern in your chest with vitality, with awareness, with intent.

Notice now that you can feel an aura of presence becoming active throughout the entire core community. You can sense this aura of presence in the extended community.

Feel the presence beginning to fill the circle of our community.

Feel the intensity and power of your presence growing stronger as it flows through the energy pattern in your upper chest.

Now focus your awareness upon one challenge in your life. Focus upon any area of your life in which you desire transformation into a new more expanded and satisfying level of experience.

Continuing to breathe deeply and rhythmically, as you focus upon this one challenge, feel the sensation of active body wisdom in your deep abdomen. Feel the power of your aspirations in the top half of your heart center. Feel presence filling you and surrounding you. Stay with this a few moments.

Notice now that you can recognize presence in each community member here.

Feel what it is to be fully recognized at such a deep level.

Notice, as you look, how powerful and appropriate this essence is, and simultaneously now, place your awareness on the point at the back of your skull where the brain and the spinal column meet. Stay with this experience as long as you like.

CHAPTER 8

PERSONAL HEALING FOR PLANETARY CHANGE

YOU are your own healing source, and the more clearly you know and experience this, the more effective your transformative work will be.

Consider the great diversity of experiences you have in your life. Consider what profound consciousness must be within you to sustain a continuity through all the various activities of your life, through the great variety of thoughts, ideas, responses, direct physical experiences, emotional and mental experiences, spiritual insights, and challenges. There is a consistent, stable consciousness within you that makes all of this possible in an organized way.

Take a moment now to consider what you feel to be the most wonderful experience of your life.

Now consider that there must be something within you more wonderful than that to have created the experience. You already have the source within you for all that you will ever create and all that you will ever do. You already have the means and the power within you for all healing and all transformation.

The healing process is a means for you to develop your consciousness. It is a cycle of transformation. Healing is far more than a problem and the various methods that are applied to it. It is even far more than what is called the cure. Because you are an integral part of the planetary consciousness, all healing as a cycle of transformation heals both the personal and the planetary simultaneously. In this time of planetary transformation, there is no distinction between personal and planetary healing.

Healing is not merely a means of responding to a challenge, not a cause and effect cycle. Healing is a means of transformation. Whenever true healing is achieved, you will know it because your life will have been changed. When you are faced with any challenge, the healing of the condition, in itself, changes you. It brings you beyond who you were before, and in so doing, it contributes to the unfolding of the entire planetary consciousness.

PLANETARY CONSCIOUSNESS
UNFOLDS THROUGH YOU.

This is why it is so important for you not to see yourself in opposition to any affliction in your life or in the world. The problem is a means for you to move into a new level of awareness and experience.

You, as personality, must remember that there is a source of your consciousness that is truly wondrous. This source of consciousness can account for anything that could be considered an affliction. It is you yourself as deep self, as source self, who have generated the afflictions and lessons of any kind in your life as a means for transformation. No matter how overwhelming or cataclysmic any challenge you encounter may seem to you, remember that you as deep self must be more powerful and more effective than whatever you are facing because you yourself brought it into your experience.

YOU CREATED
EVERY CHALLENGE IN YOUR LIFE
AS A MEANS FOR TRANSFORMATION.

Begin now to relax, and to find a pattern of deep breathing that is comfortable.

Focus your attention in upon yourself. Notice what is present within your experience.

Notice that what is active within you is exactly that force which you have used to generate all your growth and development: the growth from the moment of conception to fetus, from fetus through birth to infant, from infant through adolescence to adulthood.

Feel the presence of wisdom already within you.

This state of wisdom is constant. It existed as your identity before this lifetime and will exist after.

Allow yourself to relax deeper into this wisdom state as you follow your pattern of easy rhythmic breathing. Take a few moments for this experience.

If you wish to know who you are, learn to be aware of yourself and your world from this state of wisdom. Then knowing who you are will be the initiation of your experience rather than a goal ahead of you to be arrived at someday if you are fortunate enough to master the questions and puzzles that seem to make up your personal history.

YOU HAVE A STATE OF WISDOM WITHIN YOU THAT IS CONSTANT.

Notice the depth of your awareness that is paying attention with the wisdom already inherent within you. Do not seek this place. Simply notice it. It is not the center from which you are reading these words. It is the center from which you are feeling your own awareness of what you are reading.

Feel the way this level of your own conscious identity already present within you has a sense of presence of great meaning to you.

Notice that at this level you can simply be aware and feel. Your focus is upon your experience in the world in present time and place. Notice how you feel the energy in your environment. Notice that you feel it as though this level of awareness is a brain with a nervous system that extends everywhere within the immediate environment that you are aware of.

Become aware now that within your body at this time there is an area where you are feeling this wisdom profoundly, an area that is most directly activated with an energy as you become consciously aware of your environment from this deeper wisdom.

Begin now to focus upon this area in your body. Breathe deeply through this focus, and allow the power of your breath and your attention to clarify the direct experience of your wisdom. Stay with this a few moments.

Notice what you begin to perceive about yourself. Notice that at this level of wisdom, you cannot find answers. This level of wisdom lies beyond distinction, beyond the division of your world into questions and answers. The wisdom inherent within you is as profound as that of any teacher you could ever wish to study with. In fact, those who study best with great teachers bring this active wisdom to their teachers. It is the level of deep wisdom that allows them to learn.

Focus on any one area of your life in which you desire more profound understanding.

Take a few moments to focus upon this area of your life experience in which you desire more profound understanding. Directly perceive and feel your deep wisdom as vibration and sensation intensifying through your body.

Notice what this experience of deep wisdom understanding feels like to you.

WHEN YOU TAP INTO YOUR WISDOM,
YOU GENERATE HEALING.

Anytime that you tap into your own innate wisdom, you begin to generate healing. Through this process, we have simply focused your wisdom so that it may generate healing in one specific area of your life. You, therefore, become able to activate the processes of personal development.

When you are dedicated to the experience of wisdom within yourself and the recognition of wisdom within others, you may generate effective healing. To that degree you will begin to lose your inclination to judge others. Do not search for the wisdom within you; reach out directly from your wisdom. From this level of awareness, you no longer compare your effectiveness with that of others. This level of wisdom does not compare. Anything it encounters, it integrates with. Comparison creates separation between yourself and something else. When you recognize anything with your wisdom, you are able to integrate with it.

All the transformative work you do integrates the universe. It continually bridges gaps of separation in the universe. The greatest spiritual teachers and healers in our history have been such because they were able to integrate with group consciousness, not transcend it.

By directly experiencing your deeper wisdom, you begin to develop presence. Through the direct and sustained experience of wisdom and presence by the members of your core community, a healing climate can be created in which transformation is tangible to yourself as an individual, to your core community, and to the world community. As the community begins to sustain a healing climate, profound transformation for the entire planetary consciousness may be generated.

WHEN COMMUNITIES EXPRESS THEIR WISDOM, PLANETARY TRANSFORMATION IS GENERATED.

It is time that communities begin to generate the healing processes that are appropriate for the new reality that this planetary transformation is pointing towards. That is why it is so important to appreciate the initiatory and active aspects of healing. The healing cycle is an initiation of transformation and fulfillment.

The most powerful healing processes at this time are likely to be those that give rise to a commitment on the part of all involved to a new experience of reality. Do not seek to heal so that you will alleviate problems or symptoms. The "problem" is simply the context in which transformation is initiated. It is a gateway into the process. This is not to imply that a challenge or affliction is necessary to initiate transformation and well-being. One of the aspects of the new reality will be insistence that afflictions and problems do not need to be healed, but rather can be used for transformation. If affliction of any kind is alleviated, all involved will understand that it is simply a result of healing. The major healing processes are those of initiation; they are not simply in response to circumstances.

Perhaps you are feeling that you are not a healer and you lack creative power. You must understand how significant your impact upon your environment is. You cannot make the slightest decision, the slightest idea appear within yourself, without affecting the universe. Nothing you can do is separate from the whole. It is the nature of the individual to act within the context of the whole. The individual can never act away from the context of the whole.

You were able to create this life because you were able to create a place for yourself in the fabric of the universe. Every act, every idea, every commitment to refrain from acting, can initiate new possibilities for you and our world. The entire planetary consciousness unfolds through your every action. As you initiate personal transformation, you truly generate planetary healing.

You as an individual affect the subtleties of the process of planetary transformation. This is why you are capable of appreciating the power and the promise of healing whether or not you believe that your work can be officially identified by society as that of healer. Everyone has a role in the development of a new reality of consciousness.

EVERYONE
HAS A ROLE IN THE DEVELOPMENT
OF A NEW REALITY.

If you desire to be part of the new reality, it is not your capacity for skills and talents that you need to create. It is your capacity to continually be struck by the wonder of the creativity and wisdom that is already within your nature.

In the development of the consciousness of Humankind at this time, an awareness is beginning to arise of the next level of human evolution. This awareness includes the realization that you are able to alter far more than simply your images of yourself or the characteristic patterns of your activity. There is growing now, in seed form, the sprouting of a new consciousness that is centered in the lower back part of the human brain. It is beginning to surface among various individuals and groups. This consciousness recognizes that human consciousness is capable of directly transforming not only the inner environment, the personal identity, but also the external environment. Through the direct use of consciousness using thoughts as pure energy forms, it is possible for any dedicated, self-aware human to directly affect the patterns and the structures of the world. It is this aspect of healing, regeneration, that is being referred to in the awareness that healing is a means of transformation.

Healing as transformation goes far beyond particular issues, symptoms, and intentions. We are working directly with this aspect of healing throughout this book. The many processes of this book are designed to enable you to apply an experience of these principles to your life, and to give you, once you have had direct experience, an understanding of the working elements involved so that you may continue to initiate transformation through yourself, your groups, and the world community.

NEW CONSCIOUSNESS RECOGNIZES
THAT
THOUGHTS MAY BE USED
AS PURE ENERGY FORMS
TO TRANSFORM THE WORLD COMMUNITY.

Healing can no longer be perceived as a response to challenge. The true purpose of healing as a process is to generate well-being as a state of conscious experience. Well-being is not simply the result of healing; well-being is the heart and soul of healing. You do not need to solve all your problems individually if you are willing to dedicate yourself to well-being. As you dedicate yourself to well-being and restructure your identity, you shift all the patterns of consciousness within your system. This changes everything. Alter your consciousness and you directly alter your experience. This is the nature of healing at this time in the development of human consciousness: healing for direct transformation.

Turn your attention inward upon yourself once again now. Feel the deep wisdom within you.

Notice the part of you that already knows. This part of you knows the opportunities, the occasions, the means for transformation that you are bringing into your life at this time.

Feel the power rising up from deep within you, the power to transform through your challenges. Simply allow yourself now to begin to feel the power that flows through you.

As you consider your capacity to generate personal transformation, notice one specific focal point of power within your body that is beginning to actively vibrate.

With the power of your breath and your attention, allow this vibration as sensation within you to increase and to radiate from this power source within you.

Allow yourself now to experience the force of your own personal power for generating personal transformation for a few moments now.

Notice now, in the area of the body around this focal point of power, the shift that begins to occur.

Feel the realignment of energy in the cells of your body, the systems of your body, your emotional and mental identity, as all begin to refocus simply because of your sustained attention upon this point of power within you.

Now focus your attention upon one issue or challenge in your life for which you desire healing at this time. You will understand these principles if you apply them directly to your life. To the degree that you are willing to satisfy yourself and resolve this challenge, you can generate healing.

AN AREA IN YOUR LIFE
IN WHICH YOU DESIRE HEALING
IS AN ENERGY PATTERN THAT CAN BE TRANSFORMED.

As you continue to focus upon this issue in your life, feel the power vibrating from this power focus within you.

Through the power of your attention and your breath, allow this creative healing energy at this point to intensify even more. Stay with this a moment.

Notice how your body begins to respond, to sustain and channel through itself this newly available, intensified energy within you.

Focusing on the area of your life in which you desire healing at this time, now allow the intensified energy from this power point to flow into this area of your life and to flood it. Simply feel the flow of energy within you and think of the area of your life targeted for healing.

Stay with this awhile, and notice what begins to shift within you. This is not an imagination of energy flowing through you. We are speaking literally of energy. Everything is energy. Everything is a specific and unique pattern of energy. The area of your life in which you desire healing is itself a pattern. All consciousness patterns are energy, and can be measured through direct experience.

They are all experienced in a physical way because they are definite flows of energy. In this exercise, you have aligned the force of your own personal power for transformation with an area of your life in which you desire healing. To the extent that the alignment is strong, the pattern of your life targeted for healing is restructured and re-created.

Now, focus upon who you can be if you heal this particular area in your life experience. Focus upon who you are becoming. Stay with this experience as long as you like.

Every challenge in your life is an opportunity not only for you to have healing, but for the entire planet to evolve. You are not simply working upon your own private issues, for you exist in your environment, and the issues of your life are never totally personal. They take place in the context of society and the entire world community. The healing work that you are doing generates a resonance within the entire world community. Your healing is an opportunity to expand the whole of planetary consciousness, and this is a profound act of service.

EVERY CHALLENGE IN YOUR LIFE
IS AN OPPORTUNITY
FOR THE ENTIRE PLANET TO EVOLVE.

Group Process 8: Experiencing the Wisdom of the Deep Self

Turn your attention inward upon yourself now. Begin to relax and to find a pattern of deep, rhythmic breathing. Take a few moments to look easily and deeply inward.

Notice the presence of wisdom within you. Notice there is a state of wisdom within you that is constant. It existed before this lifetime and will exist after. Notice that this part of you knows the opportunities and the means for your transformation you are bringing into your life at this time.

Allow yourself to relax deeper into this wisdom state as you follow your pattern of deep, rhythmic breathing. Feel the power that rises up from within you, the power to transform through challenge.

Notice from this level of awareness that you are able to feel the energy of this environment. Notice that you feel it as though this level of awareness is a brain with a nervous system that extends everywhere within the immediate environment that you are aware of. Feel your wisdom as active vibration, sensation, radiating out through the environment.

Bring your awareness now to a point at the back of your skull, where the brain and the spinal column intersect. Notice how you are beginning to experience your wisdom. Take a moment to go deeply into this experience.

Notice now that you can feel your wisdom throughout your body and the space around you, and you can sense the active wisdom in those around you. Continuing to focus on the point at the back of your skull, notice that you can feel the energy field of wisdom for this core community. Stay with this a moment.

Continuing to focus on the point at the back of your skull, simultaneously begin now to breathe through your heart. Feel the active sensation, here in your heart. Now, from deep within you, feel your presence. Feel your presence beginning to radiate through your heart and align with the energy field of wisdom of the community. Continuing to breathe deeply and rhythmically, stay with this experience a few moments.

Feel the increase in energy within yourself, and also within this environment at this time. Feel the power of the community healing climate that has been generated. Feel your access to this basic lifeforce that can never be drained.

Now focus your attention upon one issue, one challenge, in your life for which you desire healing at this time. As you focus upon this one issue in your life, simultaneously feel the power vibrating throughout our community. Feel the power vibrating throughout your entire body. Allow the healing power of the entire community gathered here to begin to flow and flood this area of your life.

Notice what happens to you, who you become aware of yourself to be, as you allow yourself to bathe fully in the accessible and abundant healing power of this communtiy at this time. Dedicate yourself for a few moments now to the total satisfaction of your true needs through the healing energy in this community.

Notice now the degree to which the power has been developed and refined through this healing process. Feel the power of healing and transformation within you and all others gathered here.

Focusing now on the point at the back of your skull, become aware of all the other communities, all the other rings of light, that are involved in generating healing in the planetary consciousness.

Consider who you are becoming now, who we are becoming. Stay with this as long as you like.

CHAPTER 9

YOUR TRANSFORMATIVE ATTITUDE

THE more you are able to appreciate what initiated the desire for transformation in your life, the more clearly you will be able to generate transformation.

Often, the transformative cycle is generated by what is considered a problem, as is the case in the cycle of healing. But all that seems to be a problem is an opportunity, and it is not enough to recognize that opportunity as a path to transformation. You must also respect the causes, the factors that generate any challenge. Then you will appreciate them. You will realize that transformation is always a cycle.

The transformative cycle is a process that includes the underlying causes, the challenge, and the resolution. Each of these is equally an essential part of the cycle and must be accepted and appreciated. Your initiation into the cycle should not be generated from repulsion of the challenge, or from a series of judgments about what causes a "problem". As you appreciate the need that any problem serves in your life, you will be able to generate transformation more clearly.

Consider as clearly as you can the attitudes that you have concerning what you consider the primary troublesome challenges of your life. Consider the level of appreciation you have for what seem to be difficulties, stress, problems, or blocks.

Consider whether or not you are able to appreciate the opportunities within you without denying your commitment to resolving these potentially creative situations.

To appreciate your challenges is not to make peace with them and defer responsibility to heal. Rather, appreciation of your challenges brings the recognition that you are capable of creating massive focuses of consciousness within yourself, both as affliction and as healing.

The attitude with which you deal with your challenges directly determines the state of consciousness in which you will be able to resolve your circumstances. If you seem to have a problem that does not go away no matter what you do, appreciate the consistency and the persistence with which you may draw from this condition all that is available. It is possible to sustain a problem from which you draw nothing because you are deferring responsibility within yourself. But your attitude toward your problems will tell you a great deal about your ability to appreciate the possibilities of transformation, of growth and development, in your life.

YOUR ATTITUDE TOWARD A CHALLENGE DETERMINES THE STATE OF CONSCIOUSNESS IN WHICH YOU MAY RESOLVE IT.

Begin now to look into yourself. Take three deep, slow breaths. With each breath focus in more and more clearly upon one aspect of your life that you consider to be troublesome. Focus upon the particular issue or condition in your life that seems to demand the most healing at this time—whatever seems to be your most crucial issue—no matter what level you experience it on.

Focus upon this one issue, and consider whether or not you appreciate the presence of this challenge in your life. Do not judge yourself. Look compassionately at this issue and upon your own appreciation, your acceptance of this problem as useful in your life as an opportunity for you to be uplifted and expanded.

Breathe deeply and consider the importance this issue would have in your life if you were able to fully appreciate it. If you were to fully appreciate this condition, what significance would it have in your life? What opportunity would it create within you?

Focus now upon the area of the body or the area of your life in which you experience this challenge. Become aware that you can begin to sense the energy focused here.

Any pressing issue in your life is a high energy focus. Notice that as you focus your attention on this issue and breathe deeply, the energy in this focus of challenge begins to become active. Feel the sensation that begins to radiate from this energy focus. Stay with this experience a few moments.

Simply appreciate, as best you can, the potential of this issue. If you are able to embrace this condition in your life, you will be able to use it for transformation.

ANY PRESSING ISSUE IN YOUR LIFE IS A HIGH ENERGY FOCUS.

Continuing to breathe deeply, allow the active energy in this one issue to grow, intensify, and clarify. Notice the sensations that you are feeling throughout your body. Allow yourself to feel the power that grows within you from this point of affliction.

You may realize now that as you create healing in any aspect of your life, you are able to generate more power, more clarity, more satisfaction in your life because of the condition that you wish to heal. It is the condition of difficulty that enables you to be transformed. The challenge is an opportunity to be creative. You can accept it as such without denying any pain, any discomfort, any disease that this condition seems to generate. In dealing with this issue in your life, you can appreciate the potential without denying the reality of your perceptions. By accepting the pain as a motivation to be healed, you can clearly accept the potential of the painful challenge.

Consider the enormous creativity with which you were able to create a challenge such as this. As your appreciation grows, you will grow in amazement of your own power and your natural orientation towards transformation.

Now you may understand that the experience of healing is not totally a response to challenge or just directed at a resolution. If you consider the reality of your life, you will notice that it does not consist of beginnings or endings. It consists of constant unfolding. This is the heart of the transformative attitude.

Focus now upon your heart center. Become aware of an energy focus in the back half of your heart center. This is a point of motivating potential energy within you. Begin to breathe very gently and easily through this point. Amplify and clarify the energy here in the back half of the heart center with your breath.

Notice that the power here in the back half of your heart center continually unfolds.

Consider the back half of your heart center to be like the bud of a flower. As the power streams forth from the back of your heart center to the front of your heart center and out into your conscious identity, the bud seems to unfold and bloom like a flower. You may think of this as the difference between the potential and the open, completed expression of this power.

THE BACK HALF OF YOUR HEART CENTER IS A FOCUS OF MOTIVATING POTENTIAL ENERGY.

Continuing to intensify and clarify the energy here in the back of the heart center with your deep breathing, notice the way in which this power unfolds continuously. Feel this constant unfolding of energy within you.

Feel the waves of power that seem to flow from the back of your heart center.

Feel the power from the back of your heart center expanding into the front of your heart center. Feel this power as it flows through you.

Feel this power as it flows from your heart into the area of your chest and up into the shoulders and neck, flows down into your midsection and through the back. Feel the capability within you to continually unfold the power that radiates from your heart center, this limitless resource of power, this presence that continues to unfold.

As you continue to focus upon your heart energy, be aware of the way your life unfolds with every waking thought.

Consider now, with each breath, the way your identity unfolds in each individual cycle of breathing. All that you are continually unfolds when you are willing to express your own creative, transformative essence.

The essence of the transformative attitude is appreciation that life continues to unfold. Any healing process or cycle of transformation is simply part of that unfolding.

Focus once again upon the challenge in your life for which you desire healing. Consider your capacity to continually unfold through the means of this challenge. Follow your ability to evolve by means of this challenge, not in spite of this issue, but by means of it. Again, the transformative attitude is essentially recognizing that all consciousness continually unfolds.

Look for the identity within yourself where this challenge has a context. Find the part of you in which this condition is a natural part.

If you wish to heal, do not seek the part of yourself for which the challenge is an unnatural experience. This will defeat the purpose of the challenge, and you will not initiate a full cycle of transformation. Find what is natural in the context of any problem. Find the purpose which is served by the challenge and align yourself with that from the heart.

Consider the issue in your own life for which you desire healing. Consider what there is about you that generates this issue as a natural part of your life.

As you find this aspect of your identity, the opportunity for profound healing is yours. It is the recognition of yourself that brings you to the essence of the transformative attitude. You cannot sustain the transformative attitude—the focus upon what is natural about you that generates a challenge—without producing well-being, no matter how the conditions may change.

THE TRANSFORMATIVE ATTITUDE RECOGNIZES THAT ALL CONSCIOUSNESS CONTINUALLY UNFOLDS.

If you choose to transform in the healing process the symptoms of what seems problematic in your life, you will always be limited by what seems to be wrong. Again, the transformative attitude is the awareness that the universe continually unfolds. You, as a natural part of the universe, are continually unfolding. Whether you continue to unfold in the same pattern so as to sustain a problem or an attribute, or whether you begin to unfold in a new pattern, let your focus be on the purpose of the challenge rather than what you are removing from your life. Be aware of what growth and benefit are unfolding. It is the way of the natural forces in our world to continually transform rather than just repair.

Focus once more upon your heart center. Look inward and find your own attitude towards transformation without judgment, with simple appreciation. Acknowledge your attitude towards the purpose, the potential, and the sense of transformation in your life.

Consider your capability to embrace transformation truly and effectively. Be appreciative of what a conscious and creative person you must be to initiate any transformation, to even initiate any opportunity for transformation.

You may be aware that your ideas of what constitutes well-being have continually been changing. There are experiences that would seem to be well-being at this time in your life, that previously would not have been appropriate and would not have been experienced as well-being. Well-being is not one finite, definable state. It is a continual clarifying of your consciousness in its environment.

WELL-BEING IS A
CONTINUAL CLARIFYING OF YOUR CONSCIOUSNESS
IN ITS ENVIRONMENT.

Notice within your heart center now, as you continue to breathe deeply through this area. Notice your presence becoming active. Feel your presence—the active sensation of your essence—radiating out through your heart center from deep within you.

Feel the sensation of energy in your heart center. Feel as your presence begins to flow down through the center of your body to the base of your spine. Follow as the energy flows from the base of your spine down to the area of your feet, and now up through the heart, and out through the shoulders, and down into the tips of your fingers. Now draw the energy from the heart up through the top of your head.

Feel this energy pattern of your natural essence. Feel the essence that motivates your life, active and flowing through you.

Feel your essence, your essential identity as a self-aware spiritual being, now flowing from your heart down through the midsection of your body, to the bottoms of your feet, from your heart through the shoulders to the tips of your fingers, from your heart up through the top of your head.

Feel the power of this energy pattern.

As you align with this pattern, focus upon the challenge in your life for which you desire healing or transformation. Notice the change you begin to experience in this condition or issue of your life.

WHEN YOU RECOGNIZE YOUR ESSENCE YOU ALTER THE CONTEXT OF A CHALLENGE.

As you recognize what is essential within yourself, you are able to alter the context of the challenge. Any challenge that does not have an appropriate context will disappear. Again, everything is an energy pattern. You transform the patterns of your identity by recognizing and experiencing the flow of your own essence as active energy. This changes the part of your identity in which the pattern of the challenge is natural. If the pattern of your challenge no longer has a context to which it is natural, it can no longer exist.

ANY CHALLENGE THAT DOES NOT HAVE AN APPROPRIATE CONTEXT WILL DISAPPEAR.

You have the opportunity for this healing in your life at this very moment. To the degree that you are able to focus your attention in present time and place upon your pattern of essence aligned with your body, flowing through your body, you are able to initiate a healing cycle. This cycle of transformation or healing will lead to new levels of challenge, opportunity, and creativity.

Focus once more upon your heart center. Feel the power of your presence in your heart. Feel the awareness of your own capacity to create well-being rising within you through your transformative attitude.

For a few moments now continue to breathe deeply and rhythmically, and allow whatever degree of healing is appropriate within your life as you feel your essence flowing as energy.

Miracles are natural. They are natural experiences that you perceive through the basic essence of who you are. Use your transformative attitude to accept the miracle of your own essence. Then you will understand that you are an agent of the universal transformative force. You must begin with yourself through your own transformative attitude. This is all you need to know to generate the most effective and appropriate healing.

MIRACLES ARE NATURAL.

Group Process 9: Transforming Through Challenge

Turn your attention inward now and begin to establish a pattern of deep rhythmic breathing.

Bring your awareness to the point at the back of your skull, where the brain and the spinal column meet.

Notice the vibration, the sensation, that you are experiencing, here at the back of your brain.

Notice that from this point you can feel the collective power of this core community. You can sense the group consciousness of this community as active awareness.

Stay with this a few moments, and simply feel the perceptions, the sensation, here at the point where the brain and the spinal column meet.

Now bring your awareness to a point in the back half of your heart center. Begin to very deeply and rhythmically breathe through this point.

Notice how the power as active sensation continually unfolds from the back half of your heart center. Stay with this awhile.

Become aware now that you are beginning to sense your presence.

Feel your presence as active power now radiating from your heart.

As you continue to breathe deeply and rhythmically through a point in the back half of your heart center and feel your presence radiating out through your heart, simultaneously now focus on the point at the back of your skull, where the brain and the spinal column meet.

Feel the power of the healing climate that is being generated in this community now.

Consider now one issue or challenge in your life for which you desire healing.

Appreciate the potential of this challenge. Consider how your life will transform and unfold through the means of this challenge.

As you consider this one issue in your life, notice now any point or area within your body that seems to be a focus of energy. Notice where in your physical body you experience this challenge as a focus of energy. Simply locate the place in your body that seems to draw your attention when you consider this challenge in your life.

Begin now to breathe through this point of focused energy. Begin to activate the focus of this challenge through the power of your awareness and your breath. Stay with this a few moments.

Notice now what you are experiencing.

Notice what you are experiencing as you allow this power focus to become active, as you allow the vitality focused here to begin to flow throughout your body.

Now bring your awareness once again to your heart. Feel your presence as active power flowing out through your heart.

Feel your presence as self-aware energy flowing from your heart down through the midsection to the bottoms of the feet, from the heart through the shoulders to the tips of the fingers, from the heart up through the top of your head.

Feel the vitality of your presence as it flows throughout your entire body.

Focus once again upon this challenge in your life, and feel now as the active energy of this challenge begins to flow in alignment with the pattern of self-aware energy of your presence.

Feel the power and the clarity of your vitality as it flows from your heart down through your midsection to the bottoms of your feet, from the heart through the shoulders to the tips of your fingers, from the heart up through the top of your head.

Feel essence filling you, resonating through all the cells of your body, surrounding you, resonating through the entire community.

As you continue to breathe deeply and rhythmically and to feel the flow of your vitality and your essence, simultaneously place your awareness on the point at the back of your skull where the brain and the spinal column meet. Stay with this experience as long as you like, and at least for the next ten minutes, as you feel this healing power move through you and the patterns of your life.

CHAPTER 10

AWAKENING WELL-BEING

HEALING is extremely significant in the times in which we live, but it is also important that you be aware of what does not need healing. It is important that you be aware of what can already be a source of joy to you. A sense of clear, uninhibited joy in your transformative work will open you to the vitality of the lifeforce and well-being.

Joy is a vital passion for life. It is an experience that you can have even in times of deep anguish, even in times when you feel a great loss or extremely pressed upon. When you feel that you are being pushed beyond your limits, or when you feel despair, you can nevertheless experience joy. True joy is the willingness to be who you are no matter how you change.

To be joyful is to accept fully who you are. It is to notice who you are, and to notice and accept everything around you that is within your experience.

If you are not willing to accept your beauty, your power, your creativity, and your wisdom as being all they will ever need to be, and still continuing to grow, then you are not in joy. But you are close to joy.

To even begin to think in these terms is to be very close to joy. If you are willing to consider that you may be beautiful, you are close to an experience of deep personal joy. To accept that your wisdom may truly be profound and ageless—even if you are not sure that this is true at this time—is to be very close to joy. To realize that you may not know your power and creativity, but it is conceivable that you have wondrous power and creativity within you, is to be willing to begin to be in joy. You cannot make joy in your life; you can simply be in joy.

As you accept your capacity for joy, you accept your capacity for well-being. To be joyful is to be centered upon your own presence. In joy you know that your essence can connect with everything and everyone.

WHEN YOU LOOK
WITHIN YOURSELF WITH ANYTHING LESS THAN LOVE,
YOU HAVE NOT MET THE TRUE SELF.

Often those who wish to know themselves have joy when they begin the journey into profound self-awareness. As they continue that journey, they become weary. The seeming impossibility of the depths they wish to explore or the heights they wish to scale is burdensome. Personal development may appear to be a burden, until you finally realize that *you* are the heights to which you are aspiring. It is yourself you meet at the peak. It is yourself you meet at the depths. It is yourself you recognize, and that is the point of full awareness. That is a point of profound joy. You will feel joy and incredible love when you meet yourself in your fullness.

When you look within yourself with anything less than love, you have not met the true self. You have simply forgotten that it is yourself you are exploring. It is only when you consider the self to be something other than you, something in front of you to look at, that you can possibly have anything less than full love and total joy being yourself. To be in joy is only to know who you already are.

Even seeing the faintest glimmer of truth, power, wisdom, and creativity within yourself, seeing that you have the capacity for joy because of who you already are, is to advance the process of transformation of the entire world community.

Personal and planetary transformation are the same. This has always been true, but now it is becoming more obvious to Humankind. You cannot act in any way without having an effect on the planet. To simply raise your right hand affects planetary awareness. You may also become aware that your inclination to raise your right hand can be strongly influenced by the action of people you have never met and never will meet. All action is intertwined. You are always acting in context. You have a profound impact on the planetary consciousness when you compassionately accept yourself in joy.

Opening to the potential for healing joyfully, rather than out of a sense of obligation, allows the most vital healing processes to function with greatest efficiency. It begins to awaken well-being.

If you can live in well-being, then healing as a cycle of transformation will have a compatible place in your life. You may simply awaken well-being, and allow the force of well-being within you to eliminate whatever is not appropriate to it in your life. Any challenges that you do not need, because they serve no creative purpose in your life, will be eliminated when the force of well-being within you is determined that you experience complete awareness of your potential.

*ACCEPTING YOURSELF WITH JOY
AWAKENS WELL-BEING.*

Turn your attention inward now. Consider any area of your life, on any level of experience, that you consider to be a problem at this time. Consider one focus of attention that you believe requires healing.

Consider your experience of this difficulty. Consider the way in which you know this area to be a problem.

As you identify this problem, notice how familiar your attention is likely to be upon this troublesome area and what you feel it affects in an undesirable way.

Notice your capacity to believe that this problem, or the area affected by it, is something separate from yourself.

This is a perspective to avoid. If you locate a problem within your system, and it causes you to deal with a part of yourself—a part of your body, identity, personality, or conceptual awareness—as something separate, as something other than you, you will not be able to sustain healing. To sustain healing that is beneficial to your development of consciousness you must reintegrate that aspect back into you. You cannot generate sustained and effective healing if you separate that part of you from the rest of you.

When you draw the afflicted part into the whole of yourself and open yourself to self-healing, you may create a context in which the problem is inappropriate and cannot exist. You cannot retain a problem unless it is appropriate to your growth in some area. When you are focused upon the advantages of being whole and able to experience every part of your life as interwoven, all that seems afflicted can be absorbed by the whole that is well and refocused.

It is important for you as a personality to acknowledge that your deep self generates all your experience. All challenges in your life have been created by yourself as an opportunity for the expansion of your consciousness.

HEALING IS A CYCLE OF INITIATION FOR A NEW LEVEL OF EXPANDED CONSCIOUSNESS.

Continue to focus on this one problem in your life. Focus upon the sense of presence, the expression of the wisdom of your deep self, within the challenge. Here you will be able to produce well-being within yourself.

If you accept your problem as having presence in your life because of who you are, you have the means to generate healing. Accepting your problem as having presence allows you to experience your essence. From this experience of total essence, presence, you are able to produce any healing that is appropriate to the needs and desires of your consciousness. The presence of affliction generates the opportunity to experience well-being. But you must be fully aligned and awake to your essence to make use of the opportunity.

Continue to focus upon this area of your life, this problem, and follow your deep, steady breathing. Notice the part of you that notices the challenge. Notice the way in which you evaluate the discomfort or the threat of this challenge.

Become aware that your consciousness can be focused at a point in the center of the area of the problem. Notice what it is to see this challenge from its center.

Feel the activation of energy here at this point as you view it from the perspective of its creator. Notice what you begin to understand about the nature of this apparent problem.

Become aware now that you are beginning to feel your presence here at this point of focus. Continuing to breathe deeply and rhythmically, follow as your sense of personal essence continues to grow and strengthen in this area.

Notice that you can feel yourself as the source of essence, as a source of experience.

PRESENCE AWAKENS WELL-BEING.

Feel what it is to have your powerful consciousness centered at this point where it is most needed, as the energy continues to increase and intensify.

Continuing to breathe deeply, feel your presence, your creative awareness clarifying and growing in the center of your problem. Take a few moments for this experience.

Now consider whether or not you choose to generate healing at this point of challenge. First, look upon it from the center, and consider whether or not you have derived full benefit from this condition in your life yet. Consider whether or not you desire to further expand your experience. Consider whether or not your intention is to transcend the level of experience this challenge draws you to. Understand that this is not a decision of values ultimately. This is a creative decision. When you make this decision from your essence rather than your personality, you will know what is most appropriate. You will then be able to generate what will serve the expression of your greatest potential.

You have the ability to generate healing. Consider the ability you have already practiced in your life. You created your body, which functions in intricate and miraculous ways. You created your personality and all of your diverse feelings.

Allow yourself to consider from your presence, rather than your personality, whether you are committed to initiating a cycle of self-healing.

Look into your heart center, and accept whatever degree of intent you find.

Simply allow the power of your presence to begin to radiate more profoundly. Feel the power as sensation flowing from deep within you out through the area of the problem in your life. Feel this sensation flowing up through every cell of your body. Continuing to breathe very deeply and rhythmically, stay with this awhile.

You may make the creative decision to be well. You are the creator in this area of challenge in your life.

You must understand that all healing is a cycle of initiation for a new level of expanded consciousness. Healing never simply removes a symptom and allows you to be where you were before. You cannot generate healing within yourself without changing to some degree the circumstances of your life. All healing is an invitation to move forward to new opportunities and new challenges.

You may, if you desire, initiate a cycle of re-creation. Through the power of your breath and your focus, simply allow your essence to flood this area of concern in your life. Feel this as sensation, not idea. Notice, as the energy intensifies here, that you can feel this area being reoriented towards your well-being. Take a few moments to guide and develop this experience for yourself.

YOU CAN RE-CREATE
YOUR EXPERIENCE OF CONSCIOUSNESS
IN ANY AREA OF YOUR LIFE.

You are a creator and a re-creator. When you identify any area of problem as being within your identity in present time and place, you align with the pattern of that challenge. As you simultaneously experience your presence, the pattern of the challenge is re-created. Presence awakens well-being. Well-being provides an opportunity to reorient your consciousness in the area of challenge, to re-create your experience of consciousness in that area of your life.

Your essence can be expressed as presence simultaneously in every area of your life and generate well-being. You can live in well-being. You can live in the constant experience of your presence.

This means of awakening well-being can be applied to any area of your life. For example, consider the concept of blocks. To believe that you have blocks is to fight against yourself. It creates an internal tension. In any area of your life where you believe that you have blocks, focus upon the quality that you consider blocked. What you consider a block is simply gathered energy that is condensed and no longer fluid. If you wish to make a breakthrough, see this energy as in seed form. Allow the seed to burst open. Allow the energy and power of your own essence to flow forth like a new shoot coming from a seed to create a new plant, a new experience. Locate where in yourself this energy seems to be gathered, for such energy will always have a physical correlation. Find the place within you where potential physical, emotional, and mental energy seems concentrated and does not flow with the normal lifeforce in your body. Then allow your presence to flow through this area, and experience it directly as sensation.

THE ESSENCE OF HEALING
IS THE FORCE OF SPIRIT
AS IT FLOWS THROUGH YOU.

The essence of healing is the force of Spirit as it flows through you and everything that exists at any level of experience. You have the capacity to tap what is truly great, what can be described as Great Spirit, or ultimate essence, or universal self-aware energy, or the Cosmic Christ, and express it within your life simply by focusing on your own essence. Your presence is an extension of that universal Spirit, that Great Spirit.

KNOW YOUR PRESENCE AND ACCEPT YOURSELF
TO GENERATE HEALING.

Focus in upon yourself once again. Notice what you are feeling now that you have integrated all parts of yourself into the whole and allowed your essence to flow through your entire self. Feel the difference that you have already generated within yourself through your presence.

When you know your essence in present time and place, you can feel your presence active within and around your body. This is important because the body can best be healed through cycles of energy application that are harmonious with the bodily structure. The healing may take place over a period of days as your body learns to absorb the results without fighting against them as unusual or distressing.

Take a few moments now to experience your presence filling

your entire identity and surrounding you. You may dedicate this moment to the awakening of a new level of well-being.

When you live in well-being, you offer to others a shared experience of well-being that is healing to them. As you experience your own well-being and communicate it to others, you stimulate the potential for well-being within them. This is a very great joy.

JOY
IS A VITAL PASSION FOR LIFE.

Group Process 10: Awakening Well-Being

Turn your attention inward and begin to establish a pattern of deep, rhythmic breathing.

Now bring your awareness to the point at the back of your skull, where the brain and the spinal column meet. Stay with this a few moments and notice the perceptions, the vibrations and sensations you are experiencing, here, at the lower back of your brain.

Notice now how much stronger the shared awareness of this entire core community of which you are an important contributor feels to you.

Notice now what you are experiencing in your heart.

Notice that you can feel your place in the ring of light that is this community of consciousness.

Notice that you can feel your connection with all present in this circle of community.

Feel the flow of active energy between your heart and the heart of the person to your right.

Feel the flow of active energy between your heart and the heart of the person to your left.

Feel the active awareness that flows up through the base of your spine from the planet to your heart and continues to flow around the circle of community connecting the hearts of all present.

Notice the sense of satisfaction and joy that is beginning to fill you.

Allow yourself to feel the resonance of your joy and your satisfaction in all the cells of your body.

Notice that you can sense this joy in the person to your right.

Notice that you can sense this joy in the person to your left.

Feel the joy and satisfaction now filling this community and radiating outward.

Notice that you can feel in your heart the awareness and the shared joy of all the other core communities and all members of the world community.

Stay with this experience a few moments now, and allow yourself to fully experience shared joy and satisfaction. Notice how complete and full you feel right now, exactly as you are.

Now bring your awareness to one issue in your life in which you desire healing or transformation.

Notice that this challenge is very much a part of you now, but you can still continue to feel yourself filled with joy and satisfaction. Feel the sensation of joy filling your body.

Notice that, in your awareness, you can stand in the very center of this one challenge in your life that is part of you.

Be aware of yourself in present time and present place, observing and feeling from the very center of this one challenge in your life.

Be aware of yourself in present time and present place, feeling the satisfaction and joy that are flowing through this community.

As you continue to breathe deeply and rhythmically and to focus on this one challenge from its very center, notice that you can feel joy and satisfaction, here, in the very center of this challenge right now.

Notice that you can feel your presence becoming active, here, in the center of this one challenge in your life.

Feel the vibration, the sensation, that is beginning to grow throughout your body now.

Feel as presence begins to radiate from the very center of this challenge within you right here, right now. Stay with this awhile now.

Notice what you are feeling throughout your body as you allow your presence to flood this challenge in your life and to inhabit your entire body.

Notice the sense of well-being that you can feel flowing through you and this community.

Bring your awareness now to the point at the back of your skull where the brain and the spinal column intersect. As you continue to breathe deeply and rhythmically, allow yourself to fully experience well-being flowing through you and around you. Stay with this experience as long as you like now, and at least for the next five minutes.

CHAPTER 11

Overflowing Your Boundaries

If you wish to get the most from your transformative process, develop the quality of the process as well as the quality of any results. Your experience needs to have as much depth as possible as well as bring you from a troubled state to a state of well-being.

If you do not appreciate the depth of your experience, what meaning will the transformation have in your life except to confirm your present idea of your own limitations? Transformation is most powerful when you use it to move beyond any idea of personal limitation that you have had.

Using healing to reinforce your old idea of who you are creates only temporary gains. If you use a transformative process that heals a problem of any kind in your life to return to the life you knew before the challenge arose, you will reinforce the identity that required such a challenge in the first place.

Transformation is far more than problem-solving. Healing is not simply for repair; it is a cycle of transformation. Transformation is what you experience when you go through change without believing in problems. When the motivation for change is motivation enough, you experience levels of transformation that you cannot conceive of when you still live in a state of attachment to certain ideas or forms.

Consider your attachment in your own life. Be aware of something or someone that you would not desire to lose. Consider that object of attachment and do not condemn yourself for this attachment. Simply consider it so you can recognize it clearly and identify to yourself your own attachment.

Having focused on this attachment, now realize that there is another perspective. It is a perspective that you had before this lifetime and will have after this lifetime. Presume that you have access in some way to this greater perspective now.

Begin to consider your attachment from this other level that you may presume you already have. Consider how much everyone and everything in this relationship of attachment would benefit if this bond of attachment was broken.

Notice that from this perspective, you can realize that to break the bond of attachment is to open the channels of communication. The less attached you are to a person or thing, the more clear your perceptions about it can be, and the more clear your communication to that person or thing.

ATTACHMENTS LIMIT CREATIVITY AND FREEDOM.

Focus upon yourself and your own life. Consider what you think you would do with your life if you had no immediate attachments and were free to act in any way. Consider what you would most desire to do if you had absolute freedom to act creatively and create any reality you desire. Simply notice what you would create.

Your image of freedom and creativity is limited by your attachments. What you would be capable of doing if you transcended the bonds of attachment is far more wondrous than you could ever imagine when you sustain even the slightest attachments.

Attachments of any kind inhibit the imagination. They inhibit your creativity. They inhibit what you are capable of receiving, what you are capable of giving, what you are capable of experiencing, and what you are capable of knowing.

If you are willing to believe, even for a while as a test, that everything in life has many qualities, and you are willing to examine anyone or anything in your life as an investigation of qualities, you will begin to realize why you do not need to be attached to anyone or anything. You will begin to realize that the most profound and enduring love bonds are not those of attachment, but those of totally free flow of energy.

This is why your personal situation, and the situation of society and the planet can never be hopeless. No matter what personal or universal disaster may occur, the situation cannot be hopeless because who you are cannot ultimately be limited by any perspective. Hopelessness at any time is simply the failure to see all the qualities of any experience.

You create opposition through attachment. It is by attaching to one person, one object, or one belief, that you are thrown off balance. You oppose something only because there is something to which you are attached.

YOU CREATE OPPOSITION THROUGH ATTACHMENT.

Think about anything that you are opposed to, what you think perhaps is your moral duty to oppose.

By opposing it you strengthen and widen the gap between yourself and your self-realization. Whatever you feel morally obligated to oppose, you make stronger in opposition to you, as you weaken yourself in opposition to it. By building that opposition, you reinforce it. You limit yourself.

As you focus upon something you oppose strongly, consider what it is that you are attached to.

If you are opposed to forces that you feel could kill you, it is only because you are attached to the various forms of life. To oppose the forces of death is to mistrust life itself. Certain conditions may require change. But understand that conditions will always change. It is your degree of attachment that puts you in opposition to anything else. You cannot truly be limited except by your own beliefs. There are many ways to overflow any limitation.

Focus inward and notice within you a point at the top of your head just inside the skull, the center of the top of your brain. Notice that even as you focus in upon this point, you already tend to activate a sensation of energy.

Here at the center of the top of the head, just inside the skull, there is a point in your brain that is immediately activated by your attention. It generates sensation. It generates perceptions to other parts of your brain.

Focus upon this point at the center of the top of the brain, and begin to activate the creative energy here through your breath and your attention.

Notice what you become aware of.

Notice the way you are aware of the resonances that are carried by what you have been reading, what your rational mind describes as the unspoken message.

Notice that you are becoming aware that all you have been reading has simply implied a deeper level of experience within you. Notice the sense within you of a deeper awareness.

Feel the shift in energy that begins to occur at this point, in the center of the top of your brain. Notice that the energy here does not remain constant, but actually often fluctuates in its vibration. Notice the way in which you experience this energy in the center of the top of your brain.

Take a few moments now to breathe deeply and rhythmically through this point, and continue to focus your awareness here as you amplify and clarify the sensation of active energy in the center of the top of your brain.

Notice the vibrations and sensations that are activated within you at this point. Become aware that in this part of the brain, you are able to experience a consciousness that feels timeless and expansive.

AT THE CENTER OF THE TOP OF YOUR HEAD
JUST INSIDE THE SKULL
IS A POINT OF TRANSINCARNATE AWARENESS.

This part of the brain, when activated, tends to look directly into levels of reality that are not limited by present time and place. This is the point of transincarnate awareness. It looks as surely and directly as the eyes in your head tend to look at whatever is in front of you. Using this part of the brain, you are able to look at what is beyond your physical experience of the world and beyond your identity in this particular lifetime.

Take a moment and intensify the experience at this point to another level through your breath and your attention.

Notice now who you begin to see yourself to be. Notice that

your identity begins to expand without creating any pressure or any stress. The expansiveness allows you to go deeply and fully into yourself.

Notice what happens as you begin to release your own attachments to your thoughtforms, your energy patterns. By releasing your attachment to them, you can think them more clearly, and perceive them with more subtlety. Notice that they do not go away.

Now bring your awareness to the point at the base of your spine. Begin to activate the vitality here, at the point of physical power.

Notice what you begin to perceive about your identity patterns that you call the body. Notice what you begin to experience about your body in awareness and sensation as the point of physical power at the base of your spine is simultaneously activated with the point of transincarnate awareness at the top center of your brain.

Feel the activated energy at the base of your spine move into harmony and balance with that at the center of the top of your brain. Take a moment to fully experience this.

Notice that you do not become two identities. Instead, you are aware of the enormity, the subtlety, and the diversity of your own basic identity.

Be aware of who you are now, who you experience yourself to be at this time. Allow yourself to go into this experience deeply.

IN UNIVERSAL IDENTITY THERE IS UNION WITH EVERYONE AND EVERYTHING.

To know who you are, as a personal identity and a transpersonal identity simultaneously, opens you to universal identity. In universal identity, there is no attachment because there is union with everything and everyone. When you release attachment to either small self or expanded self and embrace both, you do not become apathetic. Rather, this experience leads you into a deeper appreciation of yourself, and everyone, and everything else.

Notice what you are feeling in your heart center. Begin to activate and clarify the energy here in the heart center with your attention and your breath. Take a moment for this.

Notice what your direct feeling is. Notice what your sensory perceptions are in the heart center. Feel the heart center opening from within like a blossom into a flower, with passion, force, and strength.

Begin to think about anyone in your life who you feel has a barrier separating his or her heart from yours. Notice that as you think about this person from your open heart, you do not need to believe in the other person's limitations. If you do not believe in the other person's heart barrier, you can reach that person's heart.

Feel your heart center now. Feel the way your energy and consciousness are active in your heart, as you realize that you can overflow any limitation, and you can do it right now.

Notice what it is for you to surrender the belief that someone, or some group in particular, is limited, constricted, and cannot be loved and appreciated for who they are. Choose someone or some group that you feel you are in opposition to, so that you may truly contribute something.

*YOU CAN OVERFLOW ANY LIMITATION
AND YOU CAN DO IT RIGHT NOW.*

To lose the idea of the limitations of others, particularly those you feel you are in opposition to, requires that you begin to lose your belief in futility in any level of your life. As best you can at this time—from your heart, from the base of your spine, and from the top of your head—help heal those that you believe you are in opposition to by releasing your belief that they are in opposition to you. Give up the belief that you cannot reach them directly.

To be a healer is simply to no longer believe in what separates you from anyone or anything in the universe.

Notice who you are that you are capable of such experience. From this level of awareness, Humankind will be able to generate more and more profound transformative activity as a community. You are now beginning to experience a level of awareness that fulfills and yet overflows the personal self. Your dedication to compassionately releasing your attachments will enhance your transformative awareness. The healing that you help to produce and the experiences that make up your lifetime can then be more fully attuned to the transformative process of the planet.

You do not lose individuality working effectively in a true spiritually aware community. Rather, you are fulfilled, and you may compassionately appreciate the diversity of awareness of which Humankind is capable.

Allow all the transformation that you have yet to experience in your world to originate within you. You are the source.

Focus in upon yourself once again. Focus upon your total self. Focus in upon the self that is heart, mind, feelings, spirit, body and personality, aura and environment. Focus upon that one identity of yours that encompasses everything that you are.

Simply be aware of yourself. And now, simply be.

Feel the ripples of energy that you are sending out in all directions. Feel yourself expanding in all directions simultaneously.

Let yourself overflow. Stay with this experience as long as you like, and notice that your own total self has no boundary anywhere.

YOUR OWN TOTAL SELF
HAS
NO BOUNDARIES.

Group Process 11: Releasing Opposition

Turn your attention inward, and begin to establish a pattern of deep, rhythmic breathing. Allow your awareness to focus on the point at the back of your skull where the brain and the spinal column intersect. Stay with this a few moments and feel the sensation of active awareness within yourself and this community.

Now bring your awareness to a point at the top of your head, just inside the skull. Notice what you are experiencing here. As you continue to breathe deeply and rhythmically, activate this point at the center of your head just inside the skull. Take a few moments to fully develop this experience.

Notice what you are feeling now at the base of your spine. Notice that here, at the base of your spine, you can feel a vibration corresponding to that at the top of your head. Notice that you can feel the harmony between the vibration at the base of your spine and that at the top of your head.

Notice that you can feel this harmony of active vibration in the person to your right. Notice that you can feel this harmony of active vi-

bration in the person to your left. Notice that you can feel this harmony of active vibration in everyone in this community.

Become aware now of what you are experiencing in your heart. Notice the sense of fullness. Allow this sense of fullness in your heart to begin to flow and radiate now.

Continuing to breathe deeply and rhythmically through your heart, notice what your direct sensation is as you feel your heart. Notice what your direct sensation is as you feel your heart center opening from within, with passion, with force, with strength. Stay with this a few moments and fully open to this experience.

Begin now to think of anyone in your life who you think has a barrier between his or her heart and yours. Notice what you are feeling in your heart now. Feel what it is to surrender your belief, right now, that someone is limited and cannot be loved and appreciated for who they are.

Continuing to breathe deeply and rhythmically and to feel your fullness and expansiveness in your heart, at the top of your head, at the base of your spine, and throughout your entire body, take an extended period of time now to individually identify those people in your life who you think have a barrier between your heart and theirs, and simply connect with them from your open heart.

Notice now the increased vitality flowing throughout your entire body. Notice the increased vitality you can sense flowing throughout this entire community. Notice that you can focus your awareness now on your total self. You can begin to resonate well-being throughout your total self.

Feel what it is to be part of this community now. Feel the active awareness and power of this community filling you and surrounding you.

Take an extended period of time now, and as a community, identify any groups or individuals that you feel you are in opposition to. Let one person at a time identify and name aloud a group or individual; let the community then take a minute or two to fully experience a connection with that group or individual through the heart. Do not rush the process. Maintain an active, forceful, open heart through your deep, rhythmic breathing.

Focus in upon yourself once again. Focus upon your total self. Focus upon the self that is heart, mind, feelings, spirit, body, personality, aura, environment, community. Focus upon that one identity of yours that encompasses everything that you are. Simply be aware of yourself. And now, simply be. Feel yourself expanding in all directions simultaneously.

Stay with this experience as long as you like.

CHAPTER 12

MOVING BEYOND SEPARATION

THE effectiveness of your transformative work depends primarily on your capacity to sustain what may be called Christ consciousness.

Christ consciousness is a state of consciousness from which you can look at all experience and all things and perceive the interrelationships. With awareness of your Christness, you perceive the Spirit force that joins together all that exists and all that happens, and you understand and appreciate the whole environment.

Your Christness is not something for you to seek. It is the expression of the truth that you brought into this world. Even if you live your entire life oblivious to the truth inherent in your nature, you nevertheless brought it into the world. It is having an impact on the world through you. In the state of Christ consciousness, you are consistently expressing your presence.

If you are unaware and unappreciative of your truth, you will find it difficult to deal with certain strong urges or drives within what you think are your personality structures. These urges can often be your truth expressing itself through you as dynamic, creative force. It will express through you whether or not you are attuned to it or aware of it. You may experience it as powerful ideas or as pure lifeforce energy. If you find that you have strong drives, urges, desires, or energy experiences that either confuse you or seem to cause a great deal of trouble, pain, or difficulty, you may be unaware and unappreciative of the lifeforce within you.

If you do not act in harmony and in appreciation with this force, many of your actions will seem traumatic and unproductive. Many of your actions may be cumbersome and painful. These underlying drives in themselves are not wrong. But it is likely, in such circumstances, that you are not perceiving the enormity of your own nature, your truth. You may not be perceiving the power that is inherent in your very existence. Your truth is a continuous consciousness; it is alive within you at this time.

YOUR CHRISTNESS
IS THE EXPRESSION OF THE TRUTH
YOU BROUGHT INTO THIS WORLD.

Truth is not something you can seek; it is your point of origin. If you have difficulty recognizing the truth in your life, stop looking for it. If what you are doing does not seem to reveal your truth, stop doing what you are doing.

You may feel when you do this, that events are passing you by. But you do not need to be a victim of these forces if you stand back periodically and see that they are recognizable currents and can be used. You can allow the forces within you to work whether or not you understand them or are fully awake to them. Simply stand back from those forces that seem to be beyond your control and begin to witness them. You will begin to understand that lifeforce energy is within you and around you. Lifeforce energy connects everything that exists and all that happens. Everything is lifeforce. Lifeforce flows as recognizable currents through yourself, society, and the world community.

The purpose of this exercise is not primarily to understand these forces. This may be the initial result, but eventually you are likely to realize that to witness the flows of universal forces, you must have your awareness centered in a particularly powerful place, your Christness. That is a place from which you can comprehend your truth. With an awareness of your truth, your life will have meaning and purpose. You will no longer believe in your limitations. It is only with your truth that you can make sense of your own personal history that will contribute to your own transformation.

There are strategies of development and purposes behind the

forces that are affecting you on many levels at this time, which can only be perceived when you step beyond a sense of linear development. Transformation is never linear; transformation is a fully expansive experience. Transformation is the experience of moving from one reality level to another. This is what is developing in our planetary consciousness at this time. By the end of this cycle of transformation, our planet will exist in a new reality.

Throughout this period, the expression of your truth will be far more crucial to you as an individual and to our planet than the movement of external events. The planet is creating a time of transformative work for the sake of expressing another level of truth. This is just as in various historic periods when the planet has shifted, sometimes through the embodiment of the work of one master teacher, and sometimes through the embodiment of work done by an entire group mind. In our present cycle, the integration of group minds will create the shift. The integration of all communities within the world community will result in the expression of another level of truth, a new reality.

THE INTEGRATION
OF ALL COMMUNITIES OF EARTH
WILL RESULT IN A NEW REALITY.

This is why it is so important to awaken community consciousness in the lower back part of the brain where the brain integrates with the spinal column. Here is the direct gate to planetary consciousness. What you are able to do with this bridge will depend entirely upon whether you bring through this gate your fears, insecurities, and wishes, or your truth as best you know yourself.

You are already a beautiful manifestation of truth. You are here, not because of what experience you need from this planet, but because of what you bring to this existence. You brought the truth with you into this plane of existence. You carry the full beauty of your spirit, your Christness, with you at this time whether or not you choose to see it for yourself or choose to express it.

As you develop the ability to perceive truth within yourself, you will perceive it easily within others. Then you will begin to move beyond the experience of separation. You will begin to live in the experience of community.

All of the pain, sorrow, and affliction you have ever experienced has come from your belief in separation. Separation is the belief, and subsequent experience, that you are separate from your source, separate from the full experience of who you truly are, and separate from the abundance that is your source.

THE ONLY AFFLICTION IS SEPARATION.

If you think that you are working hard at trying to access your "higher Self", and therefore, beginning to move beyond separation, you are affirming your belief in separation. Who is this "I" that seeks to connect with something other in order to be itself?

If you see that there is anything else that you must be to experience your wholeness, or that in just one moment more you will be worthy, you are creating the experience of separation in your own consciousness.

No matter what the circumstances of your life, you carry the full perfection of your spirit within you now. It is the power that generates your existence. It is you. Your life is simply the unique expression of what is already perfect as it continually refines and unfolds.

THE ULTIMATE EXPERIENCE OF CONSCIOUSNESS IS UNITY.
THE ONLY LIMITED EXPERIENCE OF CONSCIOUSNESS IS SEPARATION.

Within the limited experience of consciousness, there are three primary problems of individuals from which all problems arise. They are the three fundamental experiences of separation. We know them as fear, judgment, and attachment. They are the major afflictions of the three primary states of matter, energy, and consciousness.

You might resolve now to analyze yourself, to examine your life, and to fight the fear, the judgment, and the attachment within yourself. But this would be an exercise in futility. You polarize yourself to what you fight. All challenges are best healed by creating the alternative experience.

Fear is the experience of separation in the world of form. You can only fear what you feel is not a natural part of you. You can only fear what you think can somehow destroy, inhibit, or hurt your personal form. Fear is the belief in separation either in a current reality or a future possible reality in the world of matter.

When you are faced with an experience of fear, affirm your fullness, your total consciousness, your truth. Fear is simply a narrow focus upon what you think threatens you. Fear is not a focus upon the total awareness, the total abundance in the world. In the experience of fear, let yourself be aware of the choice of love, compassion, harmony, and particularly, power. It is only by going through fear to the state beyond it that will release you from fear.

The state beyond fear that will release you from all fear is the state of silence. Truth—the undifferentiated all-inclusive state of consciousness—is most easily explained as a state full of wisdom that you experience as silence. Silence is not the absence of awareness. Silence is fully integrated awareness. This means that anyone who experiences true silence engages in unity rather than dialogue with anything or anyone. When you no longer distinguish between yourself and all others, when you experience and acknowledge shared truth, you begin to experience this silence. This will transform your fear. In perfect silence, there can be no fear. Fear is a form of separation. It cannot exist in unity.

FEAR
IS THE EXPERIENCE OF SEPARATION
IN THE STATE OF MATTER.

The experience of judgment is an affliction on the level of energy experience. All of your judgments that divide the universe into good and evil or right and wrong are themselves means of limiting the options for your energy to flow.

If you find yourself with judgments, do not try to find a reason to no longer judge. Simply realize that anytime you judge, you are denying yourself an experience of the abundance of the universe for the sake of what you think is the assurance of safety. You are denying yourself the opportunity to be a full channel of creative energy.

Any distinction that you think is of value that separates one from another results in pain. Pain is simply energy that you have focused which has no clear channel through which to flow. It is the nature of energy to flow. When energy has no clear channel through which to flow, it is because your judgments and beliefs have resulted in separation and broken the circuits through which that energy may pass. If you are in pain, you know that you are somehow limiting yourself.

If you suffer from the pain of divisive judgment, pay attention. Attention is the one great response to the experience of judgment. In judgment, you simply are not paying attention to all of your experience. You are not noticing the full scope in which you are operating. It is as if you were driving a vehicle and seeing only the road in front of you and not the traffic to either side of you. You have limited your options and created an opportunity for a great deal of pain. This is one path you may choose, but you do not need to choose the path of division, of pain. You may learn to pay attention to all your life experience.

JUDGMENT
IS THE EXPERIENCE OF SEPARATION
IN THE STATE OF ENERGY.

As you read these words now, begin to pay attention to yourself. Notice what you are feeling.

Bring into your awareness the image or thought of a friend. Notice that you can pay attention to this person, and it does not matter whether they are attentive to you.

Become aware that you can be fully attentive and look into the truth within your friend. Notice that you are not affected by the personal limitations of your acquaintance.

You do not need to judge anything about your friend to know the truth within. You may understand now that if you are fully attentive to the truth within your friend, your friend's judgments will not stand between you two.

Now focus your attention upon yourself. Notice what happens as you look directly at the truth within yourself. Simply notice what you are experiencing within yourself.

Become aware of an area of increased sensation or a point

within your physical body that seems to draw your attention as you look into your own truth.

Focus your attention in the center of this area. Begin to very gently breathe through the area. Notice what begins to grow within you.

Notice that what grows within you is not in any way a new opinion about yourself; it is simply an awareness of yourself.

Notice that no matter how loudly your judgments call to you at this time, you may also experience a state of true silence. You may experience your truth.

As you pay attention to yourself in this way, become aware that you can sense a knowing within you that causes increased vitality to flow through you freely.

Take a few deep breaths and allow yourself to feel your vitality flowing from every part of your body into this energy focus and from this energy focus back into every part of your body.

As you allow this energy to flow through your body, notice that your personality and your mind begin to relax and feel in harmony with your body.

Notice how much simpler your physical experience becomes as you move beyond judgment and allow your vitality to flow throughout your entire body. Take a few minutes now to enjoy this experience.

ATTACHMENT IS THE EXPERIENCE OF SEPARATION IN THE STATE OF CONSCIOUSNESS.

Attachment is the experience of separation in the state of consciousness. Attachment is the belief that you cannot know everything, and so must know some aspects of your experience well. When you experience attachment, you are believing that only what you are experiencing directly can be available to you. All attachments allow you to experience only a part of the greater abundance.

If you are suffering through your attachment, open yourself more fully to direct experience. You do not need to have judgments about your attachments in order to free yourself from attachment. To believe attachments are now wrong when before they were right may free you from attachment, except for the attachment to your judgment. You do not need to trade one problem for another. Simply allow yourself to experience anything in its fullness. Take five minutes a day to pay full attention to what you are doing. Allow yourself, while you are eating, to fully notice everything you can about what you eat. Or in those five minutes, walk, or sit still, and notice fully how every part of your body, mind, emotional system, and aura feel.

You will begin to appreciate your fullness, your wholeness, your truth. It is the experience of your wholeness that will eliminate attachment from your life.

You can know the distinction between attachment and preference because you must surrender something to have what you are attached to. With attachment, you must deny yourself full satisfaction for the assurance of security.

BELIEVE IN YOUR FULLNESS TO MOVE BEYOND SEPARATION.

When you allow yourself to create the alternative experiences to fear, judgment, and attachment, you will know your true well-being. You will be expressing your truth.

Do not try in your life to heal your flaws; express your unity with what is flawless. Express your truth. Believing in yourself as an affliction will not serve you. It is enough to simply believe in yourself, in total acceptance of every aspect of yourself as you are now. To believe in your fullness is to move beyond separation.

If you believe that you must be healed, you will fear everytime you turn away from the active process of transformation. If you hold the judgment that you are inadequate, you will have pain whenever you relax that judgment. If you are attached to the idea that you must connect with something other than what you are now to be fully yourself, you will feel lost when you try to put the attachment to rest.

We may speak of three aspects of existence and three aspects of affliction and the greater truth to which these aspects point. Yet, you do not need to learn the aspects of existence. You do not need to perfect your way of dealing with the aspects of separation. You do not need to surrender anything of who you are. There is always the opportunity for unity through your inherent truth.

When you believe in yourself, in total acceptance of every aspect as you are now, you affirm your fullness. This is an affirmation of unity that will carry you beyond the experience of separation.

Your truth is intact and cannot be hidden from those who are willing to see. As you perceive the truth directly in all relationships, you will find that the personality, your personality and that of any other, is actually like a convenient language rather than the fullness of your experience. Your personality traits are simply the way you choose to express aspects of your truth.

If you are willing to even try to express your truth, you will not feel you need to heal your personality. You will not feel you are a victim of the personality traits of others. As you understand this, you will begin to comprehend what relationships in the new reality are about. Those who will fully profit from this new reality will be those who negotiate all experience not on the level of personality, but making use of the tools and grammar of personality.

YOU CAN UNITE WITH EVERYTHING THROUGH YOUR TRUTH.

Take a few moments now, and focus your attention on whatever there is that you can create unity with without fear, without judgment, without attachment.

Notice what happens as you begin to experience that shared source of unity. Breathe deeply and allow yourself to fully experience your truth. Notice what is beginning to happen within you.

Notice that this experience springs not from a new way of doing, but from what you feel you do not need to do anymore.

Notice that by not needing to do anything, you begin to experience the silence of your own truth. Notice that you can be fulfilled, that you can be calm, that you can be in balance, that you can be in harmony, right now, exactly as you are.

Be aware that silence fills you, and surrounds you, and embraces this entire environment.

Notice that there is nothing that you can be aware of that you cannot unite with through your truth.

You cannot create your truth. You can only continue to awaken to new levels of perception of your truth. There is no separation on this level of consciousness, and yet the full integrity of the individual is sustained. Integrity is not sustained through division; it is sustained through unity.

Feel the part of you that will never be changed. Feel the part of you that is the constant center of your consciousness.

It is the part of your identity that is the site of the experience of enlightenment. Feel your power here.

You are far more powerful when you seek anything you wish to pursue in your life from this point of consciousness than you are when you use every experience in your life to find this point of awareness. Both methods are creative choices, but only one is the choice of power. The other is the choice to believe that power is not present in you.

Feel the rising strength within you as you know the truth within you.

Feel active within you that part which understands all this already and simply makes itself available right now for an experience of your Christness. Notice what you are aware of for a few moments now.

EXPRESS YOUR TRUTH AND YOU WILL MOVE BEYOND SEPARATION.

Choose this experience not as your goal in this life. Choose this experience as your starting point, no matter what you believe to be your ability at this time.

It is the expression of your truth that will carry you beyond the experience of separation. It is the expression of your truth that contributes to the integration of consciousness on every level of reality. It is the expression of your truth that is your Christness and that makes your experience of community possible.

We are at a time in our planetary consciousness when we have the choice to believe in unity, to understand that the experience of community can fulfill the individual, and allow the individual to know itself and be at one with the entire universe.

Through this transformative work, we are all becoming aware of our unity. There is your individual consciousness. There is species consciousness. There is planetary consciousness. There is galactic consciousness. There is dimensional consciousness, and there are also levels of transdimensional consciousness in which you are already taking part.

The period we are in is a time of your participation in something much greater that personal and planetary transformation. The entire universe is cooperating in a specific cycle of transformation. It is able to do so because there is a truth that unites everything, at all times. This truth will be constant throughout this entire cycle and into all other cycles of transformation.

This truth is active in you right now. As you express it, you share your Christness.

AS YOU EXPRESS YOUR TRUTH
YOU CONTRIBUTE
TO THE INTEGRATION OF CONSCIOUSNESS ON
EVERY LEVEL OF REALITY.

Group Process 12: Experiencing Unity

Turn your attention inward, and begin to establish a pattern of deep, rhythmic breathing.

Feel the planetary awareness moving up through the base of your spine, through your heart, and out to the heart of the person on your right and continuing around the circle of this community. Feel the power of the active planetary awareness flowing through the community, becoming stronger as you continue to breathe deeply and rhythmically and to allow the power and the awareness of the planet to flow through you.

As you continue to feel the flow like a ring of light connecting all in the community through the heart, now allow the planetary awareness to move up to the point at the back of your skull, where the brain and the spinal column meet. Feel the sensation as planetary awareness continues to flow through the base of your brain to the corresponding point in the person to your right and continues around the circle of community.

Take a few moments now to increase the vibration and the intensity of both rings of light. Allow these rings to expand, and to merge, and to encompass your entire body. Feel the active awareness as sensation filling your body and surrounding you. Feel as this core community becomes a radiant sphere of light.

Notice now that from deep within every cell of your body and deep within the heart of the community, you are beginning to feel presence. Feel presence as it radiates out through the community. Stay with this experience awhile.

Now become aware that this community is resonating with many other communities of consciousness. Notice that we can feel the place of this community in a great network of interlocking rings of light that surrounds our planet. As we continue to resonate with our presence, our truth, feel the other communities with which we are in resonance. Notice that as we begin to recognize presence, truth, in other communities, we begin to align and to link with them.

Recognize presence active in all the great forests of the planet. Feel essence alive in the grasslands and the plants of the prairies. Feel attunement through essence with the plant life of the mesas and deserts, the tundras, the marshes and swamplands, the savannahs and jungles. Recognize presence now in the fruit-bearing trees, the cultivated vegetables, the family of flowers. Feel what it is for this community to resonate with the presence, the essence, of the entire community of plant life. Stay with this a few minutes.

Recognize presence in the great mammals of the oceans. Feel as we resonate with essence in the mammals of the land, the animals with fur, claws, hooves. Feel presence in the creatures of the sea and the air. Feel what it is for our community to resonate with the essence within all creatures of the animal world. Stay with this a few minutes.

Recognize presence in the great body of the planet. Feel as we resonate as a community with rock and mineral, water and gas. Stay with this a few minutes.

Feel what it is now for this community to resonate with presence and connect with everyone, everything, everywhere through the sensation of this one truth.

Feel the presence now of the great extended communities of the universe, the vertical communities that extend beyond our world. Feel what it is to be connected throughout all space, all time, through our capacity to resonate with the one shared Truth.

Continuing to breathe deeply and rhythmically, focus on the point at the back of your skull where the brain and the spinal column intersect, and feel truth active within you and everywhere. Stay with this experience as long as you like now, and at least for the next ten minutes.

CHAPTER 13

WORKING WITH FUNDAMENTAL ENERGIES

YOUR transformative work needs to be valuable to its context. If you change to accomplish the effect that you desire when that effect is not appropriate, you will experience a misalignment of your own energy.

The transformative context is not simply the environmental, or psychological, or emotional conditions that are related to your desire or need for transformation. The transformative context is your whole state of awareness as you enter a transformative cycle. Transformation exists on many levels simultaneously, and every level of the multi-level context is affected. There are many considerations. But if you are mindful of the considerations that are within the grasp of your awareness, you are more likely to create an effect that is worthwhile and leads to greater well-being.

A truly powerful personal transformation will produce a revitalized context for yourself. Such transformation will have a ripple effect upon all with whom you are in connection. Every transformation creates an effect upon the life path of everyone involved. Here you can begin to appreciate the awesome potential of the core community network that we are creating. Generating transformation through interconnected communities will have a profound impact upon our world. This can be done effectively when you are aware of the transformative context.

If you wish to transform the context, fundamental energies are extremely powerful. Fundamental energies are useful because they can communicate across several levels of reality simultaneously. The energies of sound and light, particularly, are effective.

With sound, for instance, it is possible in transformative work to generate a tone that harmonizes with all the crucial levels of the transformative context. This tone can resonate compatibly with what needs healing without disrupting other levels that do not require the direct effect of healing. Tones can be created by instruments of any kind or sung. A tone of sound generates resonance and harmony, and therefore will affect several levels simultaneously in the transformative context.

Sound is powerful because it is highly compatible with the energies within the physical body. The use of sound can generate healing that will endure. If it is possible to "retune" several levels within yourself during healing, there is less likelihood that other levels of your identity will react against the transformation.

SOUND IS POWERFUL BECAUSE
IT IS COMPATIBLE WITH
THE ENERGIES OF THE PHYSICAL BODY.

The fundamental energy of light translates itself directly into other levels from the state in which you experience it, and therefore is very beneficial to the transformative process. Light energy also has an essential vibration. In sound, it is described as tone; in light, it is termed radiance. Radiance is the essence of light manifestation. It is possible to use light to create levels of radiance that harmonize several levels of the transformative context.

Radiance and tone both have two purposes in the transformative situation. One is to harmonize all the levels of experience in the healing. The other is to expand the experience on each one of these levels so that transformation will be experienced as expansive.

So that you may understand this more fully, focus in upon your heart center. As you begin to breathe deeply, be aware of the radiance or tone in your heart center.

Simply focus upon what seems to have radiance or tone in your heart center.

Through the power of your awareness and your breath, allow the tone or the radiance in your heart to become activated.

Notice that this tone, this radiance, interacts with your environment.

Notice, to the best of your ability, the way your tone or radiance affects your environment.

Consider how the tone and radiance of your heart energy reach everyone in your environment.

Notice the impact you have upon your environment at this time simply through the energies that you are radiating from the heart, light and sound.

This is important to understand if you wish to generate effective transformation. To the degree that the fundamental energy you radiate from the heart is harmonious with your environment, you are capable of initiating transformation that is truly beneficial. It is the purpose of the transformation that is crucial. What is obvious change may not produce whatever transformation is appropriate.

Refocus your tone and radiance to positively affect the environment.

As you continue to breathe deeply through your heart center, begin to expand and refocus your tone and your radiance. Stay with this a moment.

Notice as you focus your tone and your radiance that you are having a beneficial effect upon your environment. With the resonance of a clear tone and a clear radiance in your heart center you are able to project presence. Presence itself creates healing for all those for whom it is appropriate. This is the principle practiced by all persons who seem to bless those who come near. This is the quality of tone and radiance that in itself transforms.

You are generating both tone and radiance from the heart whether or not you are aware of it. With a clear tone and a clear radiance, you have the ability to heal and transform the environment. This will do a great deal for your life and for all others who are with you. Here is the expanded sense of the transformative context: to transform as context, to heal your environment by being an active, willful, awakened member of your environment.

Transformation does not need to be oriented towards the problems of individuals, the problems of communities, nor even problems themselves. Transformation can be oriented towards the greater transformative context, the greater environment, whatever level of greater environment that you are able to perceive. It may be the space that you are sitting in, the area around you, the full landscape as seen in the distance, a sense of the entire planet, or a sense of the entire universe. You can initiate beneficial transformation on any of these levels if you can generate a clear tone and clear radiance from within you.

RESONANCE
DRAWS EVERYTHING INTO UNION.

It is resonance, the empathy of essence with environment, that can awaken Spirit within all experience. On all levels of reality, resonance draws everything into union. Resonance is simply empathy of vibratory experience. As you emit the clear tone and the clear radiance of your essence from your heart, you are in tune with and you resonate with Spirit, that essence that joins together the entire universe.

Here you will understand the way you are able to perceive yourself as individual and as part of the universal identity simultaneously. These states are not in contradiction. The resonance of two musical instruments playing notes that are completely in tune with each other does not contradict the individual nature of either instrument. Rather, it affirms the tone the instruments play. It is not simply a sound echoed back, but a tone that is shared. The tone is what is constant between them. You experience the individual and the universal simultaneously at this level of consciousness.

It is the interrelationship between your deep self and your environment that allows any transformation to produce well-being that will endure. Well-being ultimately transcends the limitations of any single, immediate environment. True well-being is the experience of what is true to all environments, all levels of reality. True well-being is the shared tone; it is the resonance of essence. In transformative work, the sense of essence within yourself and within others will give you the fundamental point of reference from which to work.

The great essence that is the core of any individual identity has the quality of multiple resonances. There is a fundamental tone of identity, but from that tone come various levels of resonance. The more refined, the more expanded and aware a consciousness, the fewer but the more powerful the specific resonances will be. The more constricted, the more rigid the identity, the greater the number of individual resonances that come from the identity tone, and yet, the less effective and expansive each of these resonances will be.

You will understand your own capacity for resonance if you appreciate that you are already by nature a resonant being. As you more fully express your essence, you change your tone. This alters the nature of your resonance. Your capacity to expand who you are and to transform your experience and awareness of your environment is then increased.

Open yourself to the resonance within you as direct experience. Hear and feel your own internal resonance as yourself, not as something for you to witness. Allow yourself to experience resonance as a resonant being.

Focus in upon yourself now. Breathe deeply and rhythmically. Simply accept for now that you are by nature a being that is already resonant. It is important to understand that you will not fully appreciate your capacity for resonance if you judge your resonance on a scale of good to bad.

YOU ARE BY NATURE
A RESONANT BEING.

The more you accept your resonance, the more your resonance will be clarified. It is not through the self-demeaning and self-criticism of your resonance that you are able to improve and enhance your resonance. You do not need to understand resonance logically if you are willing to accept it within you. Your appreciation of your resonance will draw you deeper into the tonal source of essence of which all this resonance is simply an expression.

Notice the experience of resonance and anything that you can identify of its nature within you.

Notice for yourself whether or not this experience of resonance seems to originate in any particular part of your body or aura, or whether this resonance seems to be present in all areas simultaneously. Simply allow yourself to appreciate what you learn from this without judgment.

You do not need to be focused upon your resonance for it to be active within you. Resonance is a fundamental level of consciousness. Your experience of personal resonance has always been essential to your functional identity. If in anyway it seems difficult for you to focus upon your resonance, it is only because you know it too well. For again, resonance is a fundamental process for you.

Allow yourself to know yourself from the experience of resonance rather than trying to identify resonance within you.

Notice others or objects that are in compatible resonance with you in your environment now.

Simply allow yourself to appreciate your fundamental relationship with your environment. Feel the vibratory resonance in your environment reaching you, tuning to you.

Although another person, or being of any kind, or object, may be defined by your perceptions as being outside you, nevertheless, you can bring the resonance of that being alive within you through your empathetic resonance with their tone that reaches you within. This is simply establishing a relationship within you of your tone with the tone of another. To the degree that you are able to do this, those sources are no longer known to you as outside yourself.

Relating to the world on this level assumes that there must be a fundamental level of well-being that can be reached through resonance. Here you find the process known as enlightenment.

THERE IS A FUNDAMENTAL LEVEL OF WELL-BEING THAT MAY BE REACHED THROUGH RESONANCE.

Consider again your awareness of your own fundamental resonance. Feel what is within you that is at the same time stable and active, constant and moving, this experience of resonance. Simply focus upon this in yourself quietly for a few moments.

Allow yourself now to appreciate the profound depth at which you are functioning. To the best of your abilities consider the expansive reach with which your consciousness is embracing yourself and your environment at this time.

Feel all that is in your environment to the farthest reaches of what you believe your environment to be. Feel all that is empathetic to you now vibrating within you. Feel all elements of the environment to which you are in tune active within you.

You are continually resonating with the forces of your environment. Everything, animate or inanimate, is resonant. You are stimulated in many ways by these resonances of various levels. They all directly affect your own experience of truth, what is your essence.

*THE RESONANCES OF EVERYTHING
ANIMATE OR INANIMATE
AFFECT YOUR EXPERIENCE.*

Nothing will awaken consciousness more directly than resonance. Reach the truth, that essence within another, from the truth, that essence within yourself. Find your resonance within the aspects of your own identity, within your own relationship with any other, within your relationship to the total environment, and you will generate transformation that is profound and appropriate.

Feel the most fundamental resonance that you can experience at this time. And again, experience yourself not as one who knows you are resonant, but from your own resonance. Experience yourself as a vibratory being. Now follow the resonance that seems to ripple inward, not outward, but inward to your basic truth. Allow yourself to go deeper and deeper into this experience of fundamental truth. Stay with this experience as long as you like.

You may fully realize now that essence, the truth, is within you, and it is within your environment. In your normal daily experience you are able to appreciate what appears to be outside you, around you. On the level of deeper experience, you can feel the way all these forces resonate through you, flow through you, are already present within you. You may know yourself individually, and you may know yourself universally.

As you allow the truth within you to awaken, you alter your experience of the world because you have refined your resonance. Your resonance contributes to the regeneration of the world on every level of reality for the benefit of all.

Group Process 13: Generating Clear Tone and Radiance

There is a very simple and profoundly effective way to generate clear radiance. Bring your awareness to the point at the back of your skull where the brain and the spinal column meet; focus until you feel a strong sensation and vibration. Then, simultaneously, bring your awareness to your heart and begin to breathe through it. This simple process is very effective for clarifying the transformative context on many levels. It can be used inconspicuously and easily to positively alter the environment in a short time.

For your group work with this chapter, practice this simple process for at least twenty minutes.

If you wish, you may also work with generating a clear tone in this session. This may prove to be considerably more difficult because you may need to overcome previous learning of some community members regarding chanting and sound. If you choose to work with tone, it would be a great advantage to utilize a tape such as Michael Vetter's overtones with tamboura; do not use a tape of Tibetan chanting. With a tape such as Vetter's, the group may simply join in.

To generate clear tone, the community must first select one note that is easily sung by all members. Everyone uses this as the basic note from which to generate overtones, and there should be no deviation. This simply places all personalities in agreement. Then, by sounding the basic note and closing the nasal airways and part of throat cavity with the shape of the mouth and the placement of the tongue, it is possible to generate overtones and chords on the basic note. This usually requires a demonstration and some practice before any noticeable clear overtones are generated. Changing the shape of the mouth cavity while sounding the basic note can produce various overtones. Groups who are adept at this frequently create amazing, clear overtones that seem to float about the room. Frequently, harmonies or melodies are generated that can be heard in the room above the group after participants have stopped sounding the basic note.

You may wish to explore this process of generating clear tone further after community members have experimented at home and have developed some ability to generate overtones.

CHAPTER 14

PRINCIPLES OF TRANSFORMATION

TRANSFORMATION is the way the universe develops and unfolds in all its continual perfection. As you begin to understand the basic principles of transformation, you will be able to initiate profound healing through your transformative work. In all transformative work, you are working with the fundamental flows, the fundamental intent of energy, of Spirit, everywhere in the universe.

There are three basic principles for you to understand and apply into direct practice in any transformative process.

Understand first that it is the nature and fundamental urge of consciousness to expand from the center. Consciousness does not move forward in a simple linear development. You can enhance the consciousness you have by progressing forward. A great deal of learning is accomplished in this way. But the consciousness that is unfolding expands from the center outward in every direction. The consciousness that is free to expand in every direction is the consciousness that will open to the most profound transformation.

Second, realize that it is the nature of Spirtit—energy that is aware of itself—to always flow. The energy of Spirit seeks to be everywhere in the universe at all times. Therefore, in all transformative work, let yourself be aware of the tendency of nature to be in motion. Even when you feel that energy is dense, blocked, or congested, realize that it is the nature of energy to flow. Offer energy the opportunity to flow, and be focused upon that flow, and you will further the effect of any transformative process.

Third, realize that the only constant nature of form is its tendency to change. Whether it changes quickly or slowly, all form tends to change.

When you realize that consciousness expands, that energy flows, that form changes, in any transformative process, you are more likely to produce the most effective results. Transformation is effective for those who allow their consciousness to expand, rather than train it to grow in one particular linear progression. Transformation is more possible for those who allow energy to flow and do not try to obstruct it, hold onto it, or slow it down. Transformation is more possible for those who allow their own forms to change when it is appropriate, and allow others' forms to change also. You increase the likelihood of effective transformation when you allow the universe to be in its natural state.

THE THREE PRIMARY STATES OF BEING EACH HAVE A NATURE:

CONSCIOUSNESS EXPANDS,
ENERGY FLOWS,
FORM CHANGES.

You can initiate true transformation by sitting quietly for five minutes and allowing your consciousness to expand as best it can, allowing your energy to flow as clearly as you can, allowing your form to change as is most appropriate to it at the time. If you are willing to do this, you will begin to feel the flow of energy between everything.

Each time you use these principles in your transformative work, you take yourself beyond the roles of one who heals or one who desires healing. You make it possible for others to also go beyond these roles. Transformation then is simply a creative and loving act. It is no longer an act of repair. It is no longer based on the presumption that anything is wrong. Rather, it is based on the deeper wisdom that anything is possible.

If your primary focus for transformation is upon what you consider to be your limitations—your injuries, diseases, neurosis, or psychosis—you will be experiencing these as the firm points of reference in your identity. All that is healing will seem to be unstable and elusive qualities that flow through and around those points of reference. You view your problems as what is firm. What is flexible and flowing seems distant and beyond your grasp. But you may learn to align yourself with what is fluid, what is dynamic, what evolves.

Your physical body itself is an expression of these primary forces of the universe. The physical body is in motion and is fluid. What is considered paralysis is a localized experience of inwardly focused energy. Energy is always in motion.

YOUR PHYSICAL BODY
IS AN EXPRESSION
OF THE PRIMARY FORCES OF THE UNIVERSE.

Focus in upon your physical body now. First notice the general relationship of the greater parts of your body, the arms and legs, the trunk and torso, head and neck, the total body in its broadest distinctions.

As you focus in upon your body, feel the way your energy flows through you right now.

Become aware now that there is a physical level of the mind. Notice that there is a bodymind.

As you focus more clearly on your bodymind, notice that your awareness does not discard your normal waking thoughts; it is beginning to emphasize thought as basic sensation.

Notice how easy it is to become aware of the way that you think as a body. The body does not know abstraction. The body only knows its own experience in present time and place. Focus in upon the body level of mind now.

As you become more attuned to the bodymind, notice that thinking becomes more basic and more clear.

You do not diminish your knowledge on the level of the bodymind. You simply experience it as sensation, rather than idea.

Feel the way you think in all parts of your body.

Notice that you think in sensory perceptions on the level of the bodymind. You do not make decisions here because they are logical or rational. Decisions by the bodymind are instantaneous because only one path makes sense to the body.

If you feel that you are engaged in a life of futility, focusing more clearly on your life through the bodymind will do a great deal to alleviate you of this. The body is already aware that the path is always below your feet. The bodymind has the clearest, most urgent commitment to keeping you on the path of your personal development. If it needs to create disease, or injury of any kind, to maintain that path, the body will do this. It is important to acknowledge this, and never work against your body.

Often in human development, the body is first to understand any new information, any new ideas. The body is usually the first aspect of your identity to be attuned to any new level of consciousness. This is why it is important to respect physical well-being.

Although the body seems to be limited because it is defined in specific form and appears similar to anyone else's form, it does not believe in limitation. That is why the form of the body always changes. That is why a body grows older in order to be fulfilled. That is why the various experiences of aging in the human body should not necessarily be considered afflictions. A great deal of what are considered problems of advanced age in our society are actually the commitment of a healthy individual to move beyond all limitations. The body is willing to disintegrate its own structure so that it may transcend its own limitations. Then the materials of the body return to its world to be put to additional use. The materials of the body never die.

YOU HAVE A BODYMIND.

The body has the means to create what is perfect for you. The body is wise. That is why it is so difficult for the human consciousness to transcend aging of the body. A great deal of what is considered a need for healing is simply a need for attention: a need for your attention to the potential of expansion of consciousness, a need for your attention to the nature of energy to flow, a need for your attention to the changeability of form.

Focus once more upon your bodymind. Feel the clarity of your awareness in the area of your feet and lower legs. Feel the lifeforce, the vitality of your wisdom in your feet and lower legs. This is wisdom that can only be experienced as sensation.

Notice now that wisdom is also present in the hands and lower arms. Feel the active energy in these areas.

Become aware that you can simultaneously focus on your hands and your feet. As you do, the energy vibrations in these areas come into clearer harmony. Although your hands and feet are highly specialized and highly distinct, they can be in total agreement about the nature of your identity and your environment.

Be aware of your experience of energy in the hands and feet, the lower legs, the lower arms, and also now, the area of the head and neck. Feel the bodymind in these areas being brought into greater harmony with your conscious awareness by paying attention.

Notice the diversity of function and form throughout your entire body. It is as complex and ecologically interrelated as all the regions upon the planet.

YOUR BODY IS A SELF-CONTAINED WORLD.

Become aware of your body as a self-contained world.

Feel how your body is a self-contained world, able to integrate with the world around it.

Notice the flows, the pulses, the vibratory experience of your bodymind throughout your entire body simultaneously.

Become aware that you can feel within your body the urge to evolve to a new level of consciousness.

The bodymind is a powerful ally in the cycle of transformation at this time. The entire planet is realigning its physical identity. Those members of Humankind who wish to be part of the new reality must do the same. You are a small world alive and functional in a larger world. It is a primary responsibility of all identities to function clearly and effectively in their environment.

Notice that you can sense on the level of bodymind, the awareness of the next experience of reality in the evolution of human consciousness. Feel this as sensation throughout your body. Allow yourself to go deeply into this experience for a few moments now.

Evolution is not a development from past into future, because it is the nature of consciousness always to expand. Evolution is the development of an ever-constant present. It is like the heart of a flower that is endlessly blooming.

The wisdom of your bodymind is balanced by the wisdom of your aura field. Your aura field is simply the field of energy that surrounds you and extends as far as your awareness in your environment. It is the transformative context with which we worked in the previous chapter. The wisdom of your aura field is constant. Yet, it does not directly respond to conditions or preferences. It is not a distinguishing wisdom like the wisdom of the body. It is an integrative wisdom that makes it possible for you to connect with others in the world. With the wisdom of the aura field, you perceive your experience that goes beyond present time and place.

THE WISDOM OF YOUR BODYMIND
IS BALANCED BY
THE WISDOM OF YOUR AURA FIELD.

The aura field flows through and around the body and is the context through which the physical body is able to maintain its structure and its density. The physical level is energy vibrating at a slower rate. This creates greater density, compact relationships of various energy patterns.

The aura field is always the environment in which any physical healing or transformation will ever take place. When you realize that this simple statement is practical, you will understand a great deal about transformation very quickly. The energy context for well-being is always present. It is the combination of the planet-oriented physical wisdom and the spirit-oriented wisdom of the aura field that generates well-being and transformation when integrated.

Here you can begin to understand how you can directly use the principles of transformation. You can deal with form as energy. Form changes because it is energy that is gathered.

You can truly perceive transformation when you realize that the three principles grow from each other and reinforce each other. The principle of consciousness always expanding is the creative aspect of an act. The principle that energy always flows is what is sustaining. The principle that form always changes is the re-creating or regenerating aspect of a threefold cycle of transformation. Think of these three principles as linked together to form one circular action. There is no interruption between these three forces at any point.

They flow into one another. Through cycles of transformation you are continually creating, sustaining, and regenerating yourself and your environment.

The primary intent of the physical level of identity is creation and re-creation. You are continually refining the energy patterns of your identity. The process of transformation on the physical level is to find the place within the body where the flow of energy can be released or stimulated no matter where the point may seem to be in relation to the point of affliction. Stimulate your consciousness of its ability to flow, and you stimulate your body's awareness of its own capacity for regeneration. It is the nature of form to change. You can change form in the physical body most efficiently by altering the energy patterns of your identity. This is an internal process. Any area in which the organism is prepared to be transformed is a point where there is a focus of energy that can be released or intensified. At that point, the most significant transformation can be generated.

YOU ARE CONTINUALLY REFINING THE ENERGY PATTERNS OF YOUR IDENTITY.

So that you may understand this, look in upon yourself now. Focus upon the aspect of your physical experience for which you most desire healing. Focus on the point that you would consider to be the highest priority of healing need.

Focus quietly for a few moments upon this point, and notice what you begin to experience as you do.

Now become aware of another point in your body, a different point, in which energy is beginning to build.

Begin to activate this second point through the power of your breath and your will. Do not pass judgment upon yourself as to why this particular point would be activated as you focus upon your desire for healing. Simply focus on this second point in the body and breathe deeply through this area.

Notice what you experience at this second point as the energy becomes amplified and clarified.

Notice that this point of developing energy is in some way related to the point in which you desire healing. This point is the point of greatest possibility of healing at this time. Realize this and you will realize that healing is not dependent upon affliction. It is not intended to repair anything, but to help generate new levels of transformation.

Continue to focus upon this point where the energy is increasing. This is the point within you of greatest healing potential at this time no matter what its correlation may seem to be with the point where you most desire healing. Locate the exact spot within your body that you find this point to be.

HEALING IS NOT DEPENDENT UPON AFFLICTION;
IT IS INTENDED TO
GENERATE TRANSFORMATION.

Be aware of the physical sensation of energy at this point—the relative warmth, vibration, intensity—any aspect of physical experience that helps you to identify the activity occuring here.

Notice that you can experience an intensifying of your own energy that does not contradict your health, your well-being, your physical balance, but rather develops that well-being. Any level of well-being that you experience can most likely be enhanced to another level of experience.

To whatever degree you truly desire the greatest personal well-being possible for you at this time, to that degree focus in upon this point of greatest well-being potential, this source of vibratory energy, wherever it may seem to be in your body, and radiate the energy at this point.

Notice now for a few moments what begins to happen throughout your entire body.

Notice that you can remember deep within yourself that you have always possessed this healing power, this creativity. You create and re-create continually on the physical level.

Be aware now of what is beginning to happen throughout your entire body as you generate this energy. Notice the pervasiveness of this experience throughout the various parts of your body.

Notice that you do not need to send healing energy to your hands and your feet. They draw that energy to them.

Notice that you do not need to send healing energy to the base of your spine and the top of your head, for they draw energy to them and radiate it from them.

Notice that your entire physical body is capable of inhaling and exhaling this dynamic intensified energy.

Notice that various other points in your body are resonating in harmony with the energy being generated from this one primary healing focus.

The more clearly these points are resonating with the primary vibratory point of well-being, the more there will be subtle harmonies radiating through all the cells of your body.

Feel the various harmonies resonating, at the primary point of healing focus, at the secondary areas of resonance, and in every cell of your body.

Notice that the body already knows how to resonate with well-being. Follow this experience for a few moments. Notice what you begin to recognize within yourself.

YOUR BODY ALREADY KNOWS
HOW TO RESONATE WITH WELL-BEING.

When you know well-being to be normal, no matter what the nature of your body, you are prepared for the powers that are most potent for Humankind in this time of planetary transformation.

As you continue to feel this energy radiating throughout your entire body, be willing to release any judgments of others and anything that creates separation between yourself and anyone or anything in the world. To allow yourself total well-being, you must be prepared to honor the potential for well-being within everyone.

Notice the increased vitality that begins to grow within your body as you release a sense of grievance, affliction, dissatisfaction, or denial that you associate with anyone or anything else.

The most profound process of transformation is based upon the awareness of the truth that is universal. When you are aware of the universal truth, you will always be compassionate. Compassion is not a judgment that someone is worthy of love from you. Compassion is an appreciation of everyone and everything without the limitation of judgment. When you judge, you make the energy patterns of your identity more and more rigid. This contributes to the inhibition of power, lifeforce, flowing within you. With compassion, you allow your consciousness to expand.

Focus in once more upon the energy vibrating through every cell of your body. Feel your entire body attuned to your current healing resonance. Stay with this experience as long as you like.

The principles of transformation are active within you. You are a form that continually changes without the truth of your basic identity ever changing. The truth of your deep self exists beyond form; it continually flows and continually expands.

You may use the principles of transformation with conscious awareness. When you do, you will know what you share with the world that it needs so greatly.

THE PRINCIPLES OF TRANSFORMATION
ARE ALWAYS ACTIVE WITHIN YOU.

Group Process 14: Activating Well-Being for Healing

Turn your attention inward, and begin to establish a pattern of deep, rhythmic breathing. Take a few moments to fully align as a community through the planetary awareness.

Focus now upon one aspect of your physical experience for which you greatly desire healing at this time. Take a moment to identify this one area and place your full awareness on it.

Focus upon this one area and notice what you begin to experience as you do.

Now become aware of energy beginning to build in another point, a different point, in your body. Locate the exact spot within your body that you find this point to be.

Begin to breathe deeply and rhythmically through this area of increasing sensation. Activate this second point through the power of your awareness and your breath.

Be aware now of the direct physical sensation of the energy at this point. Feel the relative warmth, vibration, intensity.

As you continue to breathe deeply and rhythmically through this second point, allow the energy to flow and to radiate. Notice for a few moments what begins to happen throughout your entire body as you radiate the energy at this point.

Notice the intensity, the sensation. Notice the consistency of this experience throughout the various parts of your body.

Now become aware that you can sense the focus of well-being in the person to your right as it resonates with you. Notice how the focus of vibratory energy within yourself begins to grow stronger.

Now become aware that you can focus this energy of well-being vibrating at different points throughout each community member. You can focus this active energy of well-being into that second point within your own body. As you do, the level of well-being energy is increased for everyone.

Continuing to breathe deeply and rhythmically through this focus of well-being energy in your body, feel now as you allow yourself to share greater well-being through others. Feel what it is to receive access to the unlimited source of well-being through others.

Notice now what is happening throughout your entire body.

Notice that you can feel healing energy flowing to your hands and feet. Feel healing energy flowing to the base of your spine and the top of your head.

Notice that your entire body is capable of inhaling and exhaling this dynamic, intensified energy. Stay with this experience a few minutes now.

As you continue to breathe deeply and rhythmically, be willing, to whatever degree you are capable at this time, to release any judgments about anyone or anything that cause you to be separated from anyone or anything in your world. Take a moment to go deeply into this experience and notice what happens.

Notice now the increased vitality that begins to flood your body as you release a sense of grievance, affliction, disatisfaction, or denial, that you associate with anyone or anything.

Feel the energy vibrating through every cell of your body. Feel what it is to have your entire body attuned to your current healing resonance.

Now place your awareness on the point at the back of your skull where the brain and the spinal column meet. Stay with this experience as long as you like, and at least for the next five minutes.

CHAPTER 15

Creating New Patterns of Experience

THE many processes of this book have shared one common purpose. They have been a means for you to refocus the patterns of your identity and create new life experiences that more perfectly express your Christness.

Anything that you can see and anything that you cannot see in your life is a specific pattern of energy. Everything—even an idea, activity, event, as well as a form—is a specific pattern of energy. By altering the energy pattern of anything, you are able to re-create your experience of it.

You are constantly doing this whether or not you are aware of it. As you consciously begin to perceive this activity, you will be able to willfully generate new patterns of experience that more fully serve you and the world. As you do, it will be important for you to cultivate and consciously refine your qualities of intent and enthusiasm.

The more you are willing to open yourself to your deeper powers, the stronger, the clearer, and the more consistent your intent must be. Intent is your will aligned with the purpose for which you created this lifetime.

You could not have been born and created the life you have now without intent. It is intent that gives momentum to your life. Even when it is uncultivated, intent can serve you in many ways, but having command over it can allow you to refocus and rechannel your energies. It is important to have a reasonable degree of command over your intent if you wish to be versatile in challenging situations. By establishing control over your intent, you can break fundamental patterns of behavior and activity in your life that do not ultimately serve you. You can create another pattern of behavior when you find yourself facing situations in which you have a familiar but discouraging response. You must first be willing to know your intent.

If you are honest with yourself for even a brief period of time, you can know your intent. If you look into anything that you do in your life, you will find that there is always one underlying intent. Your intent points directly to what you are able to gain in any situation according to who you are.

The intent with which you developed your identity during infancy, childhood, and adolescence will greatly determine the possibilities of your growth and experience. But it does not predetermine your life history. It determines the possibilities only. If you do not become so fascinated with the experiences of your lifetime that you lose memory of your intent, you will be able to take the same power with which you initiated this lifetime, and apply it directly in your life now.

If you wish to greatly change the conditions of your life, use your intent, the same power with which you initiated this lifetime. You can create new patterns within yourself. You can create the patterns that affect your environment responsibly. You can begin to reflect the fundamental pattern of your Christness.

YOU MAY RE-CREATE THE PATTERNS OF YOUR IDENTITY TO EXPRESS YOUR CHRISTNESS.

By adulthood, the specific intent by which you initiated your life may become a habit if you are not continually aware of yourself. When intent is like a habit, you live in response to circumstances. If you feel that your life is a series of responses to circumstances that are out of your control, you have accepted the habit of your personal intent. You are still working with your intent as you did through childhood and adolescence.

If you find yourself in this situation—if you find yourself

feeling that you need to manifest more, or perhaps less, in your life—it is important that first you appreciate how much you have already created through your intent. You do not need to take credit for everything, because a great deal has occurred through group agreement. But your agreement has often had as much determining weight as anyone else's, even if they seemed to be in charge. If you desire to manifest something different than what you have been experiencing, you must start with appreciation.

THE FIRST STEP
IN CREATING NEW PATTERNS
IS TO APPRECIATE WHAT YOU HAVE ALREADY CREATED.

Do not defer appreciation until you have manifested your intended result. If you cannot appreciate what you have already created, you will not appreciate what you create in the future. If you are not used to appreciating what does exist, and you create what you desire, your reaction will be to look forward to the next creation. This is an exercise in nonappreciation. Appreciating only your potential, not your reality, will stand in the way of what you might create that would truly serve you most. This is far more crucial to you, if you wish to evolve your consciousness, than creating what you think you want.

The first step in manifesting new patterns is to appreciate what you have already created, beginning with your own body. No matter what you may think is wrong with your body, it is what is right with your body that allows you to be here at all. This is the first step.

Turn your attention inward now, and begin to establish a pattern of deep, relaxed breathing. Focus upon what you have already created.

Look at the body in which you live. Do not judge it by external evaluations such as beauty. Consider and appreciate the subtlety of its function.

Be aware of all the various systems that are functioning in your body, even as you are sitting still and reading.

Notice the subtleties of your life support and life regeneration systems, for the body is your base of operations.

Now appreciate your capacity for emotional experience, no matter how varied or how unvaried it may seem to be. Refrain from making external judgments, and simply notice what you have created—the range and subtleties of your emotional experience—rather than considering pleasure versus pain. Notice both in your life. Notice the finesse with which you have refined those states. Appreciate what you have as emotional experience. Notice it in as much detail as you can.

Begin now to appreciate your mental structures and processes.

As you appreciate yourself, notice that it is not just your mental consciousness that is doing all the appreciating. Appreciation involves sensation, feeling, idea, and knowing. Sensation is the physical realm of experience, feeling the emotional realm, and so on, through the mental and spiritual realms. You appreciate from all four of these levels simultaneously.

Appreciate the spiritual level of your awareness, what can be called true knowing, that which is a pure energy state. Notice the energies that flow through you and around you.

APPRECIATION INVOLVES SENSATION, FEELING, IDEA, AND KNOWING.

If you practice appreciation with honesty, it will open you to enthusiasm. You cannot take such a detailed tour of yourself without opening to an enormous enthusiasm for your creativity.

The process of creating new patterns begins with focusing your intent. It develops through appreciation. True appreciation leads naturally to enthusiasm. Enthusiasm that follows intent and appreciation will create an expression of your greatest creative capabilities. This is why intent and enthusiasm are important qualities in our world.

Many people experience a great deal of distress because they do not feel clearly focused upon who they truly are. If you feel you have lost touch with your basic identity, consider your intent. Enthusiasm will sustain what is the best within you. The step that must be made in-between them for appropriate expression of yourself is appreciation. When all this is done efficiently and deliberately, you will create what it is that you truly need.

It is important to consider that we are not speaking here of the laws of manifestation. This is the flow of manifestation. Intent develops appreciation. Appreciation generates enthusiasm. Enthusiasm transforms into manifestation. These are not distinct steps. They are four parts of one cycle, just as the four seasons are each part of a cycle of one year. They are different, and yet, you do not experience a specific borderline between them.

If you are willing to cultivate your ability to manifest directly through intent, appreciation, and enthusiasm, you can have more creative control over your own life and your contribution to the world community. If you are focused on your greatest potential, everything that you create will be what is most appropriate for you and the world.

*THE FLOW OF MANIFESTATION
INVOLVES FOCUSED INTENT, APPRECIATION,
AND ENTHUSIASM.*

Focus your awareness upon yourself now. Relax and find a rhythm of deep, steady breathing that is comfortable.

Focus your attention upon the base of your spine. Begin to breathe deeply through this point. Allow the energy here to become active through the power of your attention and your breath. Take a moment for this experience to develop.

Notice the vibration and sensation at the base of your spine. Notice your total experience of the energy at this point for a moment.

The point at the base of the spine can be considered a point of connection between your personal intent and the physical realm of experience. If you are determined to create anything that can be physically experienced, it is usually an advantage to begin at the base of your spine, to begin at your point of physical reference.

As you focus upon the sensations at the base of your spine, focus also on one specific result that you wish to manifest, something that you will be able to experience tangibly.

As you focus upon the tangible result you wish to create, also feel the power and the intensity of the energy at the base of your spine growing. Feel the power of your intent in this project of manifestation increasing. Stay with this experience for a few moments.

Now allow your focus to rise from the base of your spine to your heart center. Focus upon what you wish to create, but also focus upon the qualities that you already appreciate within yourself that would be served by this manifestation. Do not try to manifest what will satisfy qualities that you have not developed yet, for this would be an exercise in futility. It would be like trying to grow crops without land or water.

Feel the power and the intensity within your heart as you appreciate yourself. Stay with this experience a moment as it continues to intensify.

SEE YOURSELF
FOR WHO YOU TRULY ARE
RATHER THAN WHO YOU WISH YOU WOULD BECOME.

Notice that you already have all the self-appreciation that you require to manifest what is most appropriate to you if you will only pay attention to yourself. You must see yourself for who you truly are rather than who you wish you would become. This is crucial to understand if you wish to manifest effectively and create what truly serves you rather than what generates more challenges.

Allow yourself, right now, to appreciate yourself.

Allow your focus within yourself once again to rise, now to the area at the top of your head. Feel the sensation at the crown of your head as you activate this energy through your attention and your breath. Be aware of the sensations and perceptions that are produced as you energize, activate, and increase the power at the crown of your head. Notice what you experience at this point for a few moments now.

Notice that your self-awareness is building. Notice the enthusiasm for whatever it is you truly need to manifest.

From here you can see its greater purpose in your life. You can see the way it can truly serve you. You can know the greater results that you can expect, that you can anticipate, that you can determine from the application of your intent.

Notice that your enthusiasm comes not only from your idea of who you want to be, but from knowing who you already are. Feel your enthusiasm here, at the top of your head for who you already are.

Enthusiasm regenerates and increases your energy. It gives you the passion to create the conception for whatever it is you desire to manifest.

Feel the intensity of the power and the enthusiasm at the crown of your head.

ENTHUSIASM COMES FROM KNOWING WHO YOU ALREADY ARE.

Now allow your attention, which carries with it your intent, self-appreciation, and personal enthusiasm, to focus upon your hands and your feet. Notice that you can maintain your attention on both of your hands and both of your feet simultaneously.

As you focus upon your hands and feet, be aware of the physical experience that you will have when you manifest the results that are most appropriate to you.

Be aware that you will create the results that will directly express your intent, your appreciation, your enthusiasm, and your receptiveness to manifestation.

Feel the center of your hands and feet vibrating with an intensified energy.

Begin now to sense that the manifestation is created, a new energy pattern has been created in your identity. Notice your physical experience around and throughout your entire body.

A NEW PATTERN EXPRESSES AN AWARENESS OF YOUR POTENTIAL.

This process of manifestation is independent of any analysis of motives, and needs, and so on. All the inherent qualities that must be addressed in manifesting exist in their pure form in this process of manifesting. You do not need to distract yourself with questions of why and how. These are the areas in which you create limitations upon your creative process. When your intent is clear and dedicated, when your appreciation comes from the honesty of self-love, when your enthusiasm comes from the wisdom of your own potential, when the manifestation exists as an awareness of the potential of yourself, the so-called hows and whys of this process prove to be limited perceptions that produce limited results.

When you are determined to express the best of yourself you reflect more of that part of you that exists beyond your personality. You begin to create something that overflows the boundaries of your own presumed limitations.

Use manifestation to satisfy your potential, not just your hunger and desire. Your potential always leads you beyond the border that you have created between yourself and the rest of the world.

EXPRESS WHO YOU TRULY ARE
AND YOU WILL MOVE BEYOND YOUR OWN
PRESUMED LIMITATIONS.

Group Process 15: Creating a Pattern of Prosperity

Turn your attention inward and begin to establish a pattern of deep, steady breathing.

Bring your awareness to the point at the back of your skull, where the brain and the spinal column meet. Feel your connection with the planetary awareness. Feel your place in this community. Feel your place in the world community. Stay with this a few moments.

As you continue to breathe deeply and rhythmically and to focus on the point at the back of your skull, consider how much you have created in your life. Do not judge yourself according to what you feel you have not done or any standard of success or failure; simply appreciate what you have generated. Appreciate how much you have created through all the cycles of your life.

As you continue to focus on the point at the back of your brain, appreciate how much Humankind has created in this world. Again, do not judge; simply appreciate, remembering that appreciation involves sensation, feeling, idea, and knowing. Simply consider how much Humankind has created in this world.

Now appreciate your place in the human family.

Bring your awareness to the base of your spine. Begin to breathe through this point and allow the energy here to become active. Take a moment to develop this experience.

Notice the vibrations and sensations here, at the base of your spine. Now send a stream of energy from the base of your spine to the corresponding point in each community member here.

Notice now what you feel. Notice the increase in the vibration, here at the base of the spine.

As you continue to feel the power and the intensity of the energy at the base of your spine growing, consider your capacity to create greater abundance and prosperity in your life. Stay with this experience a few moments.

Now allow your focus to rise to the area of your heart center. Feel the active vibration and sensation. Send a stream of active energy from your heart to the heart of each other person in this community.

Feel the increase in the vibration, here in your heart center.

As you continue to feel the power and the intensity of the energy in your heart center growing, consider the qualities that you already possess that would be served by manifesting greater abundance and prosperity in your life. Stay with this experience a moment as it continues to intensify.

Allow your focus once again to rise, now to the top of your head. Feel the sensation here, at the crown of your head, as you activate this energy through your attention and your breath.

Notice your enthusiasm for manifesting increased abundance and prosperity in your life. Notice that you can see its greater purpose in your life. You can see the way it can truly serve you. Feel your enthusiasm for who you are.

Now send a stream of energy out from the crown of your head to the corresponding point in each other community member here. Notice what you are experiencing. Notice the increase in power at this point. Feel the intensity of power and the enthusiasm, here at the crown of your head.

Now allow your attention to focus on your hands and your feet. Notice that you can maintain your attention on both of your hands and both of your feet simultaneously.

As you focus upon your hands and feet, be aware of the conscious physical experience that you will have when you manifest the results that are most appropriate for you.

Now bring your awareness once again to the point at the back of your skull where the brain and the spinal column meet. Consider the physical experience that Humankind will have when it manifests the capacity for abundance and prosperity that is appropriate for the world community. Stay with this experience as long as you like.

CHAPTER 16

REPATTERNING

YOU can change your experience on a personal level, on a social level, and on a planetary level by regenerating the energy patterns of consciousness.

A great deal of your experience is created as a result of the transformation of your identity patterns. You can learn how to consciously transform your personal identity patterns. You may re-create the pattern of any part of your body or any belief that you hold. This changes your experience. Through community, you help re-create the patterns of consciousness of society and the world community. All new experiences and new levels of awareness are generated off patterns that are related to other patterns in the world.

You may be feeling that the subject of regeneration is too complex or abstract for you to grasp. You may doubt that you can apply it in your life. You must understand that you have already proven your capability to consciously regenerate the energy patterns of your experience. The many processes of this book have guided you through the experience of consciously regenerating the patterns of challenges in your life. Through the group processes, you as a member of the larger community have been actively regenerating patterns of consciousness on the social and planetary levels. You have already proven your capability.

Now you may allow your rational mind to understand what you already know on other levels, instead of being an agent of limitation to you. Often, it is your rational mind that tries to define what is possible and what is not possible for you without the benefit of experience. In this way, the rational mind can limit your experience. But now you must understand that the experience of regeneration is possible for you, because you have already created it.

For true regeneration in any area of your life, call upon energy patterns of something you associate with the experience that you desire. You do not need to use only those energy patterns that are at hand, that seem to be within your own biological or psychological structures. You can adapt or use any energy pattern in the world around you. You can begin to alter your energy patterns directly and regenerate the life awareness within yourself simply by focusing upon objects whose qualities offer you a great deal.

YOU CAN USE
ANY ENERGY PATTERNS IN THE WORLD
TO RE-CREATE YOUR IDENTITY PATTERNS.

For example, if you wish to develop an identity more like that of a tree—to be solid, stable, well-grounded—focus your entire awareness, your intention and your will simultaneously upon that tree. Focus upon it until you begin to sense the energy pattern within that tree.

The pattern is contained within every cell of the tree. The pattern itself has a deeper identity that reflects into the cells. The pattern is more fundamental than simply a genetic code. The genetic code itself is an extension, an elaboration, of this basic pattern.

Focus upon the tree and as you become aware of its energy pattern, you will sense within yourself the vibration of the energy pattern of your own deep self. Enter into a state of harmonized energy with the tree. You are then able to comprehend the qualities of the tree through direct experience.

All basic concepts have energy patterns. It is not only those things that crystallize into form that have patterns. Every concept is a very specific, identifiable energy pattern with a structure as specific as any molecular order. By focusing upon the energy pattern of a concept—not the form, or word, or name, but the sense of something within the concept that is more fundamental than language and structured form—you begin to understand more fundamentally.

So that you may more fully comprehend regeneration, turn your attention inward upon yourself now. Begin to establish a pattern of deep, steady breathing.

Focus on a point directly in front of the center of your brain, and begin to breathe through this point very gently. As you do, allow the power of your attention and your breath to amplify and clarify the energy at this point, directly in front of the center of your brain. Take a moment to develop this experience.

Become aware of the vibratory sensations that are being generated in this part of your brain.

Feel what it is to sense the energy vibration of your own consciousness at this point.

Continuing to focus on this point, just in front of the center of your brain, simply allow the energy at this point to continue to grow.

Be aware of the sensation of thought within your mind. Feel what it is to truly experience the energy of your consciousness as vibration.

Through the power of your awareness and your breath, continue to amplify and clarify the energy, here just in front of the center of your brain. Stay with this a moment.

A POINT
JUST IN FRONT OF THE CENTER OF YOUR BRAIN
INFLUENCES YOUR PERCEPTIONS.

Within this part of the brain, there is a point of energy that directly influences your interpretation of all perceptions that you receive from the world.

As you become more sensitized to the power at this point, notice that there is an origin to the vibration. The focused power at this point has a source.

Notice that you can begin to sense the source of this vibration, a source so deep within your consciousness that it seems to be more fundamental. Allow yourself to experience a sense of this source of consciousness. This is the source of the way you interpret and synthesize the information you receive about the reality in which you function.

Feel deeper into this vibratory point. Notice a sense of an energy pattern.

Notice that you can follow the vibration here, just in front of the center of your brain, to its very source. Notice how easily your awareness flows into this source. Here at its source, this energy is in itself a gateway to unlimited awareness.

THE REALITY
THROUGH WHICH YOU MOVE
IS VIBRATING ENERGY PATTERNS.

Your perceptions of your reality point in both directions. As you look outward, you as deep self see the reality through which you are moving with your perceptions. As deep self, you deal with reality to the degree that the sensations and perceptions of your personality are open and appreciative of experience.

There is much that you as personality perceive that you do not seem to use directly, but you as deep self experience through those perceptions. The reality through which you move—in its essence, vibrating energy patterns—is flowing through your perceptions into your deep self. Your deep self, which is more fundamental than your personal identity of this lifetime, draws in information and experience through these energy patterns. You as deep self use the perceptions through these energy patterns to create the patterns of your identity and to interact with the reality through which you are moving.

YOU MAY WORK ON
THE LEVEL OF PATTERN AWARENESS
TO TRANSFORM YOUR WORLD.

Your physical identity has energy patterns. Your emotional and mental identities are derived from energy patterns. The concepts and principles with which you deal and interact with the world are also energy patterns. By working directly on this level of pattern awareness, you are able to refocus a great deal in your world.

These energy patterns are regenerative because they focus both ways, to your deep self and to the outer world. They are active points of transition of transformation. As you alter your energy patterns according to your needs, your will, your focus and intent, you transform profoundly. Through this process you magnify your presence because you allow your deep self to actively express your lifeforce. That is why self-awareness is a regeneration process on the level of these patterns.

SELF-AWARENESS IS A REGENERATION PROCESS ON THE LEVEL OF PATTERNS.

It is not what is new that is often needed, but what is sleeping in the consciousness of yourself and the world that needs simply to be regenerated, and thereby awakened. If you wish to truly expand your consciousness, you must be aware of your consciousness and intend to apply it directly to the consciousness within everything around you.

You may interweave your identity with the patterns that constitute the world. This is possible because all energy patterns vibrate. As patterns interact and harmonize, they create resonance. The interaction of your deep self, through your waking identity, with the common reality through which you move is an active continuous interplay. Through this interaction of basic energy patterns, you transform on fundamental levels. You can use this power for personal change. You can use this power for social change. You can use this power for universal transformation and enlightenment.

Focus now, once more, upon the point just in front of the center of your brain. Allow the energy at this point to intensify.

Feel yourself within the energy pattern of your consciousness at this point just in front of the center of your brain, the point at which you interpret and synthesize your responses to the reality in which you live.

Now focus upon a concern in your life that is a major challenge to you. Think of this concern from the point just in front of the center of your brain.

Feel what it is to stand in the center of the energy pattern of your concern and be surrounded by the energy vibrating from it.

Now become aware that you can sense your deep self within the pattern of your concern. You can feel your presence.

Continuing to focus upon the concern in your life, begin to focus inward through the point just in front of the center of your brain. Focus toward your deep self. Allow your conscious awareness to be a direct bridge between your deep self and your outer concern.

Now allow your concern to flow into this point, here just in front of the center of your brain, to where you strongly feel your presence.

Feel as this energy pattern is revitalized and refocused by the profound awareness of your deep self. Feel the sensation as this energy pattern is literally refocused. Feel the power of your presence vibrating in this point, just in front of the center of your brain, as you continue to simultaneously focus on your concern and your presence. Stay with this awhile.

Notice the reorganization of this energy pattern. Be aware of the shift in vibration, in radiant energy, that is appropriate to you.

You started at the pivot point of change, at the point just in front of the center of your brain. You reorganized and refocused your comprehension, your appreciation, and your intent through this energy pattern. You refocused the energy pattern of a concern in your life by directly aligning it with the energy pattern of your deep self, that part of you that knows your purpose and extends beyond lifetimes.

YOU REFOCUS THE ENERGY PATTERN OF A CONCERN BY ALIGNING IT WITH THE PATTERN OF YOUR DEEP SELF.

When you regenerate an energy pattern, you reorganize your capacity to know. Any analysis you make of information, concepts, or experience will be made in terms relative to the energy pattern.

Energy patterns are the basic creative tools of the deep self in active consciousness. As you maintain flexible and strong energy patterns, you have the capacity to be a source of change, rather than a servant of change. The most profound change that you can make is a change in your own consciousness. All of your experiences depend upon the state of your consciousness.

Feel again the sensation of vibrating energy in the point just in front of the center of your brain. Feel your presence.

As you feel your presence strongly, allow it to flow. Allow the aware energy from the center of your brain to flow outward through the front half of the brain to the forehead and out into the world. Feel as you generate a series of self-aware energy patterns. Notice the intensity of the concentration that transcends a sense of limited awareness. Stay with this awhile.

Consider again the concern that is most appropriate to you, but now, focus upon your new relationship with this concern. Feel the intensity of focused concentration as you direct energy through the front half of your brain into the world. Stay with this awhile.

Notice your active interaction with what you are confronting. Your relationship with any concern joins you with the energy pattern of that concern. You have the capacity to change your own energy patterns so that you are now more aligned with what you are focusing on. The pattern of anything that you focus upon can be re-created as you create resonance with your choice of focus.

YOUR RELATIONSHIP WITH A CONCERN JOINS YOU WITH ITS ENERGY PATTERN.

Feel your deep self awareness surfacing in the front half of your brain. Feel your presence.

Now focus upon your heart center. Notice that there is a corresponding energy pattern here in the heart. Activate this energy through the power of your awareness and your breath.

Notice the affinity between the energy pattern of consciousness in the heart and those you have generated in the front half of the brain. Notice your capacity to focus the consciousness of energy patterns at both these points. You can profoundly expand your awareness of who you are as you are able to know your own wisdom, the truth of any concern, on several levels simultaneously.

Notice now, as you focus upon the front half of your brain and your heart, that you are generating self-aware energy patterns throughout your body and aura. Feel other parts of you becoming alive and aware of themselves.

When you are aware that you are aware, you create a circuit of consciousness that expands your capacities to awesome levels. Feel your capacity to resonate with awareness throughout yourself.

Notice your awareness in the front half of your brain and in your heart center. Be aware that you are aware.

Feel the shift in your own identity. Feel your capacity to expand your creativity through this practice.

Focus upon a point now approximately a hand's length above the top of your head. Notice how you feel as you refocus your awareness of yourself at this point simply by directing your attention to it.

Feel your awareness active in this point, above the top of your head. Feel yourself being aware of yourself being aware. Stay with this awhile.

Notice the shift in your consciousness.

Feel yourself aware of yourself now above the top of your head, in the front of your brain, and in your heart. Feel the truth of your awareness at these three points simultaneously.

Now consider one area of your life where you desire transformation. As you focus upon it, feel your consciousness shift.

Feel the shift in your self-aware energy patterns at these three points.

With focused attention, with focused appreciation, and with focused intent, you are able to create what is most appropriate to you in this area of your life. As you initiate a process of regeneration, you do not need to experience it all at once. Many processes of regeneration have their greatest effect over time.

Feel your profound regenerative force awakening within you. Feel your presence.

Allow yourself to be focused upon the truth that is the source of your regenerative power. Stay with this experience as long as you like, and understand that it is your truth that allows you to continually regenerate the patterns of yourself and the world.

YOUR TRUTH
ALLOWS YOU TO CONTINUALLY
REGENERATE THE PATTERNS OF YOURSELF
AND THE WORLD.

Group Process 16: ***Repatterning***

Turn your attention inward, and begin to establish a pattern of deep, rhythmic breathing. Bring your awareness to the point at the back of your skull, where the brain and the spinal column meet. Take a few minutes now to activate this point and to feel the awareness of community consciousness.

Now focus on a point directly in front of the center of your brain. Begin to breathe very gently through this point. As you do, simply allow the energy here, just in front of the center of your brain, to grow. Take a moment to develop this experience.

Feel the sensations of energy vibrating here in your brain.

As you become more sensitized to the power at this point, notice that you can sense an origin to the vibration. Notice that the focused power at this point has a source.

Notice that you can feel the source of this vibration, a source so deep within your consciousness that it seems to be not fully within time or space.

Notice that you can follow the vibration here, just in front of the center of your brain, to its very source. Feel how easily your awareness flows into this source. Feel yourself now within the energy pattern of your deep self.

Focus now upon a concern that is a major attention in your life.

Feel what it is to stand in the center of this energy pattern and be surrounded by the energy vibrating from this point.

Now become aware that you can sense your deep self within the pattern of your concern. You can feel your presence.

As you continue to breathe deeply and rhythmically and to focus upon this concern in your life, allow your awareness to go deeper into yourself and to focus on your deep self. Feel your presence.

Feel your awareness as a direct connection between your concern and where you strongly feel presence, here deep within a point just in front of the center of your brain.

Feel the sensation, the vibration, as the energy pattern of your concern is literally refocused by the profound awareness of your deep self.

Feel the power of your presence vibrating in this point, just in front of the center of your brain, as you continue to focus simultaneously on your concern and your presence. Stay with this experience awhile.

Notice now what you are feeling. Be aware of the shift in vibration, in radiant energy, as this energy pattern is reorganized.

Feel the sensation in the point just before the center of your brain. Feel your presence.

As you feel your presence strongly, allow it to flow from the center of your brain outward through the front half of your brain to the forehead and out into the world. Stay with this awhile.

Now focus upon your new relationship with your concern. Notice your capacity to change your own energy pattern so that you are now more aligned with that upon which you are focusing. Simply focus on your new relationship with your concern.

Be aware of the sensations, the perceptions, the shift in consciousness that you are feeling inside your brain.

Notice how self-aware you are.

Notice yourself being aware in the front of your brain.

Notice yourself being aware in your heart center.

Notice yourself being aware a hand's length above the top of your head.

Feel your awareness throughout your entire body. Feel active awareness around you and filling this community.

Now consider one area of your life in which you desire regeneration. As you focus upon it, feel your consciousness shift.

Feel presence radiating from you. Feel the power of presence flowing through this core community, radiating throughout the entire world community.

Now bring your awareness to the point at the back of your skull where the brain and the spinal column meet. Stay with this experience for as long as you like, and at least for the next five minutes.

CHAPTER 17

THE CURRENT OPPORTUNITY

YOU have the opportunity to begin to experience yourself in a new way in this time of transformation. If you choose to do so, you may open your awareness to an experience of a greater sense of self. You do not need to go far to make the most of this opportunity. In fact, if you are determined not to go far from where you are, you will realize what you already have. You will realize who you already are. You will know what is already possible.

Let yourself simply explore what is possible. Our entire universe is transforming. We are creating all of this together. Your role is as valuable as that of anyone else. Through group cooperation, we are all learning and transforming. As one community we are re-creating the patterns of our world to reflect the fundamental pattern of the Cosmic Christ. We are beginning to live in an emerging new reality.

Do not wait to prove to yourself what is possible. This is not necessary. Through your transformative attitude you know that consciousness is continually unfolding, your life is continually unfolding. Through your continuous consciousness you know that there are no beginnings and no endings, only ever-expanding cycles of transformation. Your belief in yourself has a great deal to do with determining your ability to perceive what your opportunities are. Again, let yourself simply explore what is possible.

You have an opportunity to continue your exploration and development through a core community, as together, we create a network that will serve as a vehicle for the Christ. The core community network is a means for group cooperation. It is a context for regenerating the patterns of consciousness on social and planetary levels through resonance with the fundamental pattern of the Cosmic Christ. It is a means of access to greater focused power of transformation for each of us in our personal lives as we each realize our Christness through compassion.

The materials of this book have been presented to provide you with basic tools with which to begin to consciously regenerate consciousness on the personal, social, and planetary levels. In a sense, learning the basics of regeneration through this book is much like learning the notes and scales on a piano. Now you have the fundamentals with which you and your community may begin to create your own melodies and music. You do not need to continually practice the processes in this book, although you may, if you choose. Once you truly grasp the fundamentals, you can create your own processes according to the creativity of your core community. There are countless effective processes that may be created, utilized, and shared with other communities. As long as they are in tune with the intent of the extended community of transformation, they contribute to the symphony that we are collectively composing.

THIS IS A TIME TO TRUST WHAT IS IN YOUR HEART.

This is not a time when you necessarily need answers. If you notice, the greater challenges in your life are not likely to go away simply because you have answers. It is the nature of challenge in this time of transformation to challenge you to be at your best. No matter what difficulties you are encountering, the challenge to you is simply to be at your best. The challenge is to live fully in the belief that you can be fulfilled and satisfied right now, exactly as you are.

This is a time to trust what is in your heart rather than what merely seems reasonable. This is not a time to deny reason, but this is particularly a time to experience your own convictions that seem to go beyond reason. Reason is a tool for maintaining a functional, effective consciousness. Reason is one way of responding to the world in which you live so that you know where you are in your world. But your journey here is not just to know your place in the world. Your life's journey is ultimately to experience recognition of your own true possibilities in a universe that is filled with possibility.

This book would never have been written had the author been reasonable. There came a time when the inner promptings were so strong that I simply had to move beyond reason. In what seemed to some an awesome act of irresponsibility, I left my job and home to begin this project with no visible means of support. The process had its moments of doubt. At a low point when I was convinced my demise was imminent, I had an experience that made me remember.

THE UNIVERSE CAN CARRY ALL OF US
TO GREATER FULFILLMENT
AS WE ALLOW
THE COSMIC CHRIST
TO EXPRESS THROUGH US.

I was writing a section on integrating communities within the world community. Suddenly, I got up, went to the kitchen, found the largest pot in the cupboard, and went out into the hot, desert afternoon. I had been staying on the edge of a lake, but the drought and the desert sun had long since taken half the lake. I walked quickly through the sagebrush and began to cross the dry lakebed heading toward a small pool, the only remaining water in half the lake.

The pool was filled with fish. The water was hot. Most of the fish were floating on their sides, gills gasping into the desert air. I began to fill the pot with fish. Throughout the afternoon, I carried pot after pot of fish from the tiny pool across the dry lakebed to the cool water and the freedom of the lake.

Eventually, I stood surveying what remained in the pool, two energetic fish that I could not catch and many dead ones, floating belly-up with eyes glazed.

"Is there anyone else who wants to go to the lake?" I asked aloud. In what was an amazing sight, a little silver fish with a blue stripe down its side literally jumped out of the pool and landed at my feet. I picked him up, and we went to the lake.

In the morning, I returned to find the two fish I had failed to catch the previous day. They were lying side by side in the mud, still living. I scooped them up and carried them to the lake, where they swam away.

Then I remembered.

To those fish I was a miracle. There was no reasonable way for them to survive. There was no rational and practical way for them to leave that pool and reach the lake, and yet they did. If the universe could create a miracle for those fish, it could for me, too, and for Humankind, and for planet Earth. The universe can lift and carry all of us to more expanded experiences of satisfaction and fulfillment as we allow the Cosmic Christ, as compassion, to express through us.

THIS IS A TIME
WHEN THE GREATEST BELIEF
IN THE WONDER WITHIN YOU
SERVES YOU BEST OF ALL.

Transformation will always seem impractical when your loyalty is to circumstantial experience alone. At this time of planetary transformation, you can make the most of the opportunities that you desire, not just the opportunities that you feel are practical. Transformation is only practical to those who can live beyond circumstances. Transformation becomes extremely desirable when you wish to move through circumstances rather than be limited by them.

This is a time when the greatest belief in the wonder within you serves you best of all. Your greatest trust in what is already true within you will help you begin to shatter your limitations. You do not need to struggle with all of your issues. What you can experience at this time of transformation takes you to new levels of realization. You cannot step knowingly into a new reality by solving all the problems in your current reality. Many of the circumstances that you perceive as difficulties can be put down and left behind like clothing you have outgrown.

When you fully experience who you are in the present—without need to go into the future, without needing to go into the past—you begin to experience fewer needs and fewer limitations. It is in the present that you can be fulfilled, and only in the present. It is in the present that you can resolve anything, and only in the present. It is in the present that promises become tangible. It is in the present that dreams become livable. It is in the present that your presence is available to you.

If you could learn only one thing from this book, understand that as you experience your presence you transform and regenerate all the patterns of your identity to more perfectly express your Christness. When you live in your truth—express your essence in the present—you contribute to the transformation of the world community so it may reflect the Cosmic Christ.

THE COSMIC CHRIST
SHINES THROUGH THE WORLD COMMUNITY
WHEN YOU EXPERIENCE
YOUR PRESENCE.

You do not need to be limited by who you thought you were. You do not need to overcome personality challenges to be transformed. Overcome your need to resolve everything, and you will begin to live in a new recognition of who you already are.

You will begin to recognize your own Christness. You will always need to cope with details that are currently meaningful in your life. But simply to resolve problems does not change the inherent truth of your life. You can change the circumstances of your life, or you can change the very process of your own perception. To alter the process and the very mechanics of your perception is to have the ability to create a great deal of change and satisfaction. It is to have the ability to perceive the deeper truth in your own potential.

WE ARE MOVING INTO A NEW REALITY
NOT SIMPLY A NEW AGE.

If you are dedicated to believing in your greater potential, you will be well prepared for the challenges that come in a time of planetary transformation. You will not be discouraged by anything that happens. You will learn how to move through circumstances rather than to just deal with them. To do battle with circumstances in a time of planetary transformation is to commit yourself to change. But to move through circumstances is to commit yourself to transformation.

Again, this time of transformation is not intended to solve the problems of society. These problems are inherent in our current state of consciousness. These problems are not the primary challenge. The primary challenge in the world community is to move to a new state of consciousness. This is why we are moving into a new reality, not simply a new age.

THE PRIMARY CHALLENGE IN THE WORLD COMMUNITY IS TO MOVE TO A NEW STATE OF CONSCIOUSNESS.

The challenge is to use both the apparent problems and the apparent solutions in such a way that the energy of both is refocused and regenerated as a new conscious experience. This is why the many processes of this book have emphasized that the problem is the gateway into the transformative cycle. The problem is as valuable as the solution in a cycle of transformation. When you embrace a problem, which has its own unique energy pattern, and align it with truth—the fundamental energy pattern of essence which is constant—all of the available energy is regenerated into a new conscious experience. This sounds abstract. This sounds theoretical. But you have experienced this practical process of regenerating the energy patterns of consciousness throughout this book and your work in your core community.

The new reality is possible for all who desire it enough to be dedicated to their own fulfillment. Do not desire only to create a new world that is more livable. Do not desire simply to serve others. Do not sacrifice your own best interests for the needs of others. Desire to be fulfilled, and you will find the new reality. This is crucial to understand. Personal and planetary transformation are one and the same. You contribute to the planetary consciousness. If you are not willing to create what is fulfilling for you, you will never contribute fulfillment to the world in which you live. What you create in your own consciousness is your contribution to the planetary consciousness. Your commitment to your own satisfaction and that of others will ultimately make the difference in your role in this time of planetary transformation.

If you deny yourself, you give up the very lifeforce with which you can serve, heal, and love. When you deny yourself, you turn away from what is truly sacred within you.

In this time of transformation, the reasonable may seem to change and become unreliable. What is truly sacred will remain constant. What is sacred to you is what joins together the entire universe. The sacred within you does not exclude anyone or anything from your love. To the degree that you embrace the sacred in yourself—dedicate yourself to what connects you with everything and everyone—you are committed to transformation and fulfillment. To be dedicated is enough. It is your devotion that makes possible the realization of who you are.

This is a time when your dedication to your true potential gives you access to what you need and also to what you desire. It is your openness, rather than your courage or certainty, that proves to you what is possible.

Love first, and then you will understand how loving you can be. Be loved first, and then you will know what it is to be loved. When you express the truth of who you are, you overflow your fears.

LOVE FIRST.

When you define and judge yourself, you see who you are not. You see your doubts. If you can measure your identity—see that you are not who you wish to be yet, see that there is anything that you are not good enough at yet, see or feel somehow that there is more you must do to do well—you are measuring your doubt and not your truth. This is not your identity. These are simply ideas about identity that are in no way a reflection of you. Doubt can be measured; truth cannot. If you have any belief in lack or inadequacy, you are not facing your truth.

The areas that you doubt are areas where you can love. If you doubt that you are capable enough in what you do, do what you do with a great deal of love. Do not be any more capable than you can be while being totally loving.

When you experience the world directly from who you are,

every circumstance is a means to immediate fulfillment. This is simple to understand. It is only when you try to make it complex that it becomes difficult to comprehend. If you wish to live beyond pain and separation, all you need to do is look into who you are and be satisfied directly by who you are as you are. Even if you think that in just fifteen more minutes you will finally be acceptable, you are creating an infinite gulf between yourself and your self-realization. All that is needed is one act of total self-compassion.

The new reality is already within you. We truly are our world, and we are receiving the Cosmic Christ. We are creating all of this together, and it is a very great wonder.

What we are creating you can feel right now if you desire. What we are creating is available to you as a simple act of total compassion for yourself that overflows into an experience of total compassion for others. There is no stress and no anxiety in total compassion. One moment of total compassion will generate a state of knowing that you can sustain always, everywhere.

THE NEW REALITY
IS AVAILABLE TO YOU AS A SIMPLE ACT
OF TOTAL COMPASSION.

If you are willing to look at yourself now for who you truly are, you will recognize something that is more apparent to you than ever before.

Live and create in this, and you will know what it is to truly give and receive love. You will know the nature of community. You will understand that compassion is neither the giving of love, nor the receiving of love. Compassion is the sharing of love. In a state of compassion, you can share yourself with others to the fulfillment of all.

Then you will understand something that goes even beyond your place in a new world community, even beyond a time of planetary transformation, even beyond a new general level of reality. You will go beyond any boundary you could ever conceive. And you are likely to be surprised that this going beyond all you ever knew proved to be the simplest thing you have ever done.

Let yourself be. You may use the core community network to share the celebration of who you already are, who we already are, and to explore our continual unfolding into new challenges and new experiences of satisfaction and fulfillment. We have the opportunity right now to receive the Cosmic Christ. We have the opportunity right now to allow the universal forces of transformation to lift and carry us through the power of our own compassion.

Group Process 17: Continuing the Work

Dear Friends,

Thank you for sharing in the adventure of transformation through this book.

We are entering a period of history when the greatest potential for both personal and planetary transformation is within group cooperation. This book has been an introduction to group work which will ground the new energies that are now beginning to manifest on Earth and result in a new reality for the planet and all the creatures that live upon it.

I urge you to continue to work through the experience of community, for there is much that can be accomplished through such group cooperation. Your community may actively participate in earthservice, and the Karuna Foundation is continually developing materials for this group work. A next book, *The Earthservice Book,* builds upon the experience of *Receiving the Cosmic Christ* and teaches groups how to work with the global chakras for planetary transformation.

I invite you to share your comments and experiences with me. Your community may contact me through the Karuna Foundation, and I will share with you the ideas and materials for this continuing community work:

Karuna Foundation
P.O. Box 11422
Berkeley, CA 94701-2422
USA

Thank you for participating in this great work of service as together we open to our collective Christness and build a new world community that embodies the consciousness of truth and compassion. Many blessings to you.

May we awaken to the compassion that we are,

Shahan Jon